Vicky Pattison is a genuine Geordie Girl, born and bred in Newcastle. Her autobiography, *Nothing But the Truth*, was a #1 *Sunday Times* bestseller and remained in the Top Ten for seven weeks. In 2015, Vicky won the nation's hearts and was crowned Queen of the Jungle in *I'm a Celebrity . . . Get Me Out of Here*. Vicky is a trusted voice on social media, where she shares personal and powerful messages about self-acceptance, compassion and self-love. She is also the host of the hit podcast 'The Secret To', where Vicky interviews celebrity friends, chatting about their secrets and sharing her own.

# Vicky Pattison

# THE SECRET TO HAPPY

SPHERE

SPHERE

First published in Great Britain in 2022 by Sphere
This paperback edition published in 2023 by Sphere

1 3 5 7 9 10 8 6 4 2

Copyright © Vicky Pattison 2022
Edited by Sarah Ivens

The moral right of the author has been asserted.

A CIP catalogue record for this book is available from the British Library.

ISBN 978-0-7515-8470-7

Typeset in Baskerville by M Rules
Printed and bound in Great Britain by Clays Ltd, Elcograf S.p.A.

Papers used by Sphere are from well-managed forests
and other responsible sources.

Sphere
An imprint of
Little, Brown Book Group
Carmelite House
50 Victoria Embankment
London
EC4Y 0DZ

An Hachette UK Company
www.hachette.co.uk

www.littlebrown.co.uk

For Paul,
Who always believed in me and somehow, even though
you aren't with us anymore, inspires me to be a better person
every day. I miss you, friend, forever and always.

# Contents

# Introduction

*Without the rain, we wouldn't feel grateful for the warmth of the sun.*

Right, guys. Before we go any further here, I want to let you all in on the biggest secret of them all – there is no secret to being happy! And I know what you're all thinking: 'She's a fraud!' 'She's a liar!' 'The cover says you have all the secrets!' But please, before you all demand a refund, allow me to explain. The reason I can't prescribe a one-size-fits-all answer – which actually may be the ultimate secret to happiness in itself – is because happiness is subjective. It looks and feels completely different for everybody, and the journey there is different for everyone. I am *so* not qualified to tell anybody how they should be living their lives, so if you're looking for a book packed with rigid rules, laws or commandments, this isn't the book for you. What this book *is* is a bit of a trip down memory lane, a recap of all the moments (and all the mistakes) that have helped make me the woman I am today – by no means perfect, but a work in progress who feels happy every day. Not all day every day, mind you – show me a woman who says they're happy all day every day and I'll show you a liar!

This book is chock full of all the lessons I've learnt from *Geordie Shore* in my twenties, of break-ups with fiancés (on television, I might add), of patching up relationships and binning the bad ones, of winning *I'm a Celebrity*, then figuring out who I wanted to be. This book is full of lessons learnt about grief, mental health, social media, and how health and diet affect our moods, our self-worth, and how we see ourselves in the world. It's about family resolutions and ups and downs with friends. My life will be very different from yours, but I'm hoping by sharing my stories, you'll feel understood, supported and empowered, and they will help you get to grips with what's going on in your life, either in the past or right now. I've had my fair share of ups and downs, I feel like I've lived, and if there's anyone out there feeling like they're going through things on their own, or they don't quite have everything figured out while everyone else around them looks like they do, or they're worried that they're not achieving what they should be, or feeling or looking how they should, I want this book to let you know you're not alone. None of us have got it figured out, not even me – who had the fucking cheek to write this book!

I've learnt the hard way that part of being happy

is embracing the journey, the imperfect. There is no end destination where you get to tick a box, and say 'I made it, I'm perfect and I'm happy and I'm always going to stay that way. La la la la la laaaaaa.' I've read quotes that state happiness is like a leaky tyre. It deflates every so often, and you need to pump it up with what it needs to stop it deflating, then keep going. I can see that! Every step of the way, every mile travelled, each ebb and flow that pushes and pulls you, is part of that journey to accepting yourself – and you need to go with it rather than fight it. Perfection isn't real, it's a construct. If it was real, we'd never feel good enough. It's when you let go of that desperate search for perfection that you can truly start to live, and to feel a sense of happiness and gratitude about who you are and what you've got.

I want a grazed knee. I want a mysterious leg bruise every so often. I don't mind a spot every now and then. I want a gravy stain on my trackie bottoms. I want a hangover occasionally (although not too often, I couldn't cope!). Sometimes I want a good whinge about my period. Sometimes I want to be sad because I miss my mam. I want all these things because all these things remind me I'm human, and they help me value the good times. To see the contrast between light and shade, and to appreciate the difference. If you don't have the grazed knees, the bruises and the hangovers, or a day when you have bad skin, you might not appreciate the days when you wake up with a clear head and clear face, or the days when you finally get to be with your mam. I want these things in my life because I think a little hardship makes us more grateful for the good times. This book isn't going to teach you how to have only light days – that's not fucking possible! – and even if it was, would you really want that? I don't know about you, but I like being reminded to be thankful for what I do have. I like that every day I'm learning and growing and improving.

## Let's be real

I spent so long hating who I was. I really did. I spent so long having other people hate me, too. For such a long time, during my twenties in particular, I was lost and confused, and inauthentic. That Vicky was stagnant, defensive and angry. When I started wanting to be better, I began to clearly see what I wanted out of life, and I recognised the things that most women not only want but deserve: a nice partner who isn't going to hurt them, a home they feel safe and secure in, good relationships with friends and family, and the ability to look towards the future with positivity. So I made a conscious decision to try and be better. And for a while, it was really hard. I'd spent so long being a rubbish version of me, being bad Vicky. It was a real effort to change. But the more time I spent being patient, and being kinder, and actually showing up for myself and giving myself a bit of love, the easier it got. And I stopped being so hard on myself, and subsequently, this version of me I've got now, after years of hard work, was built and added on to, and made to feel right. Made to fit. The authentic version. The real me.

I let go of feelings of anger, and hurt, and those memories and resentments from things that happened to me ten years ago. When you let go of the past, all the stuff you've been beating yourself up about fades away and you can start afresh. I think once I stopped raking over the coals of my life, I was able to focus on who I could be and unlock my potential, and then it became the easiest thing I've ever done to be authentic and embrace unapologetically who I am. Which, by the way, is a total fanny. But now I own being a total fanny. Some people might think I'm super strong and confident, but I'm actually a really vulnerable and sensitive person, and scared a lot of the time. Oh my god, I'm literally always terrified, but I'm not afraid to admit that to anyone now. You know why? Because we all are deep down. And why wouldn't we be? Life is fast and confusing and unpredictable, so it's understandable that we'll feel hesitant from time to time.

I struggled for so long to find the best version of me

that now I'm fiercely protective of her, and you best believe I'm never going to lose sight of her again. I encourage readers of this book to keep sight of their authentic self, as well – because it's in authenticity you can finally like who you are, even love who you are, whether you're alone with your thoughts, surrounded by friends or in a crowded room full of strangers. And that is a pretty amazing feeling.

A word of warning for all you reading this and hoping to embark on some personal improvements: some people don't like it when other people get healthy. People noticed the change in me, sometimes before I noticed it in myself, and their reactions told me a lot about their intentions. When you start to make positive changes, you'll work out who isn't in your corner, and who is. For example, my mam recently told me she was grateful for the relationship we have now.

'I've always loved you,' she told me, 'you've always done things that impressed me, like going into the jungle and getting out of your comfort zone, but sometimes I didn't like you very much. But now, who you are growing into makes me really proud to be your mother.'

Granted we'd had a couple of drinks, but I do feel a drunken person's words are a sober person's thoughts, and her telling me she'd noticed all the work I was doing showed me she was paying attention; it reminded me just how much she cared.

'People always used to tell me you were clever when you were at school, and you could do anything you set your mind to, and it was nice to hear but it never impressed me. Now, when I hear you're polite or kind, that makes me proud because that's a decision you've made. Being clever isn't a decision. You're choosing kindness.'

It meant a lot to me that my mam noticed this person I was trying to be, that I was slowly becoming. I'm doing it for me – you have to do it for you, you can't do it for anyone else – but it's lovely to make a positive impact on others too. You don't work hard to buy a nice house to sit in it on your own; you work hard so your friends can come round to that house and have fun, and you work hard so you can take your mam on holiday, and you work hard so your sister doesn't have to worry about money all the time. When people start to notice changes you make, it makes it even more worthwhile.

## Ignore the idiots

There's obviously the other side, when sometimes your personal growth and achievement holds a mirror up to other people and shows them what they're not doing, and it can get quite ugly and dark. I'm lucky I've got good friends, and they all seem content to let me shine. They're happy with what they're doing, whether it's getting promoted, having babies, getting married, or just still figuring it out. They can be supportive of me and feel happy for me, and vice versa. But I do see jealousy and envy, especially on social media, from people who want to remind me of who I was ten years ago and the decade of drama I've been through publicly, be it my weight fluctuations, my tumultuous relationships with friends, family and lovers, or the mental health issues that followed my fame, and the criticism and attention it brought. They want to humiliate or insult me because of them. But I, and you, have to learn to ignore these idiots who want to pull you back into being that lesser version of yourself. Don't let them make you doubt yourself. Don't let the fact that they're intimidated by you stop you shining. You've got this.

I know I've come on leaps and bounds, and I am a new person. And some people don't like that. They are the people who are insecure in themselves and want to keep you down to make themselves feel better. Do not give in to these people who don't have your best interests at heart. Cut them out of your life if possible because they don't deserve you. They are not able to keep up you with as you go forward in the positive direction you're headed, so they'll try and dissuade you from forging boldly on. Only take the good, supportive, encouraging people with you on your journey. They are the ones who deserve to be along for the ride.

## Help yourself

This book isn't here to tell you what to do – I mean, following my escapades might help you realise what NOT do to – but ultimately, it's here to make you feel better when you have gone ahead and done the things everyone told you not to do, and their warnings come true, and you feel silly or sad or have a head full of regret. I am here to say, 'Don't worry, you're not the first and you won't be the last, pet, you're not alone.' I want this book to feel like a hug. I want you to read this book and know I've been there, I understand you and I'll be your mate. This book can be the place you come where you know you won't get judged. When your mates are sick of hearing you've got back with that toxic fella for the thirteenth time, and thirteen was unlucky after all (who knew? I mean, EVERYONE! But we move on . . .), I'm going to tell you it's all okay, and that nothing you've done is irreversible. Believe me, there's nothing you can do that is so bad that I haven't done worse. I've designed this book to let you know that we're all a bit fucked up, and we're all still figuring it out. We all travel at our own pace, facing speed bumps and twists and turns, but we can keep going. I hope you'll work through my stories and misadventures and realise you're not the only one who's had a shit day, a shit boyfriend or a shit job.

We need to support each other, and to understand there is not one blueprint for life, or a right or wrong way to live. For so long, I was made to believe that if I didn't have a partner, or I didn't have kids, or if I didn't have a dream wedding, then I wasn't a success. It didn't matter how many television shows I did, or how many fitness DVDs I made, or books I released, I felt everyone was looking at me like I was a sad, single girl who couldn't keep a fella. And I don't want any other woman to ever feel like that. Success, to me now, is being happy, content and liking who you see in the mirror, and that doesn't come from having a fella, or having loads of kids, and it doesn't come from having loads of money either – it comes from working on you and embracing who you are, whether it's your little boobs or your massive bum, your impatient side or your terrible timekeeping.

If you want to be the cool aunt or uncle and not have children of your own, that's amazing. If you want to be a hippy parent who doesn't believe in using deodorant, and has a million kids running around with no shoes on, you do you. If you want to be a badass CEO and order around a staff of 200 people, fucking get yours! Just try not to look at someone else and be jealous of what they have, or judge them for what they haven't done, or feel inferior because their life highlights in some painful way what you think yours is missing. We're all different, and it's taken me thirty-three years to work this out. I don't have to have a partner and loads of kids to be whole. But I have to be authentic, and kind – to myself and to those I love – and I have to believe that the more I grow, and learn, and stop trying to be perfect, the happier I will be. And I'm so glad you're here on this journey with me.

# 1

# Finding your feet in your pesky, pinot-filled twenties

*Don't panic, don't rush, don't force anything.*
*Soon you'll be the person you deserve to be,*
*with the right people alongside you.*

I have always been driven and focused, scarily so. If you speak to my mam about it, she's guaranteed to bring up this one moment in my life when I was about eleven years old – a story I find super embarrassing but she absolutely loves it. It's the tale of when she caught me doing an extra-curricular school project about safety in the science lab, and I can remember it as clear as day – and not just because she won't let it go but because it is burned into my memory as the moment I realised my mam thought I was a nerd. Our science teacher had been telling us off that week because everyone was being careless and reckless, not focusing enough on being careful with all the equipment in the lab, and he was at the end of his tether. So he said, 'If anyone wants to write an essay about how you should conduct yourself in here, you'll earn extra credit.' And of course, I rush home, turn on the computer, and sit there working away while all the other kids are out in the street playing and having fun. I'm writing this essay – not for school, just because I want to do it – and my mam comes in, can't believe her eyes, and takes me to one side to teach me about the importance of switching off and letting loose, lecturing me on how I needed to go out and make friends, reminding me that I was a kid.

At the time I remember thinking, *bore off and let me write about Bunsen burners, mam, I could be saving lives here!* But it was such a pivotal moment in my life. My mam still says, 'If I knew what you were going to turn into during your teens and twenties, I'd have encouraged you to keep writing that essay.' Bless her, if only she'd known what was coming.

It was just the way I was, though; I was born with a razor-like focus. Even from eleven years old, I knew what I wanted out of life and I knew I was going to get it. I wanted to be successful, but I suppose my idea of what success looks like changed a lot over the years. It's still changing as I get older. When I was eleven, success to me was simple. I wanted a life like my mam and dad had, I wanted a job and I wanted to be good at it, and I wanted a husband, kids and a nice house. A sweet little life. When I turned eighteen, success looked like a nice car, a designer handbag and dating a famous footballer. (Cringe, I know! But can you honestly tell me that you didn't become obsessed with the idea of becoming a WAG after you watched Victoria Beckham and Cheryl Cole at the 2006 World Cup? I rest my case.)

But let's be clear: I didn't want to date the footballer for his money. No matter what age I was at, and whatever goals I had, one thing has remained constant: I have always wanted to make my own money and to be able to look after myself. Probably inspired by the strong women in my family, I've never wanted to rely on a man. I just knew that the idea of asking a man for anything didn't sit well with me and I wanted to be self-sufficient. By the time I was eleven, I had a paper round. Granted, my mam did most of it, bless her – another fact she doesn't let me forget: 'You did it for about two weeks, and then there I was, driving around in the car with you.' By the time I turned fifteen, I worked in Shelly's Shoes, and at sixteen, I got a job in Kookai, which made me feel like the duck's nuts. I got 50 per cent off, man! My point is, even from an early age, I always wanted success and independence, in whatever form it took at the time, whether it meant being able to buy my own shoes and handbags as a teenager, or being able to help support my family as an adult.

## The university of life

When it came to choosing my college degree, my
mam gave me some sound advice. She said, 'Choose
something you love, because if you don't love it you
won't go. It doesn't matter to us what degree you get, as
long as you're enjoying it.' I love theatre: Shakespeare,
watching plays, the costumes, I just love the drama
and magic of it all. So I chose to take drama, media
and cultural studies and I have never regretted it once.
I loved it and have some of the BEST memories from
uni. I worked hard, as driven and determined to suc-
ceed as ever, and was juggling three jobs at the time.
But I played hard, too (obvs). I chose Liverpool John
Moores University because it wasn't far from home but
mostly because I wanted a Scouse boyfriend – I really
loved the accent and they're so much fun. Although,
you know what, I never bloody got to kiss a Scouser
the whole time I was there! Aside from that, I'm so
pleased I chose Liverpool. It's such a fun and vibrant
city and the people are so warm and friendly – a lot of
similarities to Geordies, if I do say so myself.

But despite all that, getting a degree didn't work
out how I thought it would. Little did I know I was
going to be leaving university the year that there'd be
300,000 graduates applying for only 30,000 graduate
jobs. In short, I was totally fucked. The market was
over-saturated with us, and I had no prospects. I was

terrified. Suddenly my mam's advice about choosing something I loved didn't seem so wise and I wished I had chosen something more vocational and job specific. I just assumed I'd work hard for my degree and get to graduation day, chuck my cap up in the air, and I'd be so sought-after in my field that someone would literally walk out of the crowd, shake my hand and offer me a great job, exclaiming 'You're exactly the person we're looking for!' Like out of a film! If you worked hard and were focused, a job would come your way – that's what I'd been led to believe. But it wasn't true. All those other graduates I was competing with were also hard-working and focused and had some seriously useful degrees, whereas mine – I mean, what was mine useful for? One of my modules was a three-month-long course on the art of mime. Who in their right mind was going to employ an amateur fucking mime act? I'd had a great time, made some incredible friends, learnt how to budget and how to do my own washing, but I didn't come out of there in a good position to face the world. I was naïve, skint and starting to get scared.

**Returning home**

Unsure of what to do next, I ran straight back home to Newcastle with my tail between my legs. I moved back in with my family and got a part-time job in G-Star, a very cool jean store in the city that was frequented by loads of lovely-looking lads, including all the guys who worked the doors at the coolest local bars and nightclubs, who'd always ask if I wanted to get my name down on any guest lists. I thought I'd played an absolute blinder. I had some luck with all my part-time jobs to be fair, and it was fun, but I did feel a bit like I was scurrying home under a cloud of shame, having failed to stand on my own two feet and secure a job. Here I was, back under my mam and dad's roof. It was difficult because after three years of uni – when you don't have to come home at a certain time, and you can eat pizza for breakfast, and if you want to bring a boy home – there's no one there to judge you. I was having to abide by their rules, which was good and bad I suppose. All of that university life thing is amazing, but it is hard, too. I have memories of stealing toilet rolls from bars because I'd run out of money to buy my own. I used to live above a bar, and come the end of the week, I'd go there to buy a burger and a beer for a fiver (which apparently I did have money for) and go into the loo and steal the toilet tissue. And when you've done that for three years, it starts to take its toll on your soul. Back in Newcastle, I remember thinking, *I'm just coming home for a few months. I'll save up enough money, and then I'll move to London.* And I believed it. As a student,

I'd toyed with the idea of being a journalist and becoming the London version of Carrie Bradshaw. I imagined that at this point in my life I'd be this sassy writer, living a fabulous life and influencing an entire generation of women with my witty and salacious words, wearing Jimmy Choos and having sexy and adventurous encounters with mysterious and handsome fellas. Instead, I was living back home with my mam and dad, in my childhood bedroom, Blu-tac still on the walls from my Take That posters, and a 1 a.m. curfew – not striding around Piccadilly Circus in my tutu, inspiring a nation of women. You've got to admire that naïve confidence you have in your twenties, haven't you?

But, wouldn't you know, I loved being back home. I'd missed my mam, and my sister, who had grown up so much while I was away. She had a boyfriend with a car, a job, and lots of Vivienne Westwood handbags (which she kindly let me borrow sometimes). She was no longer just an annoying little sister, but a really fun and cool person who I wanted to spend time with. Honestly, I just loved her so much. And being back at home, where there was always a fridge full of food, was a dream. I suppose it was the little things about being home I had missed as well. You'll never underestimate the value of a spice cupboard after you've been away to uni. Before you go, you never give your mam's spice or baking cupboard a second thought. If you need oregano or flour, you just know it's going to be there. But when you go away to uni, and you don't have those things, you start to realise it takes years to build up a good spice rack. I came back and everything was there, and – I know it sounds so silly – but that oregano brought me such comfort. I have never taken oregano for granted ever since.

What I'm trying to say in a herb-heavy way is that I just loved being at home. But I got too settled and for the first time in my life I stopped being this really excited, driven person. I'd really pushed myself at uni, to go somewhere new and try something new, and meets loads of new people, and I'd thrived, but I was tired. When it hadn't worked out how I planned it in my head, the prospect of putting myself out there again scared me. What do I do now? Do I have to be skint again? Where will I get my oregano if I leave? I was so comfortable and relaxed being at home that I allowed my ambition to fade and stopped looking towards the future, which at this point was a bit of a mystery to me. Living day by day like this was a slippery slope. Weeks turned into months, and as I sunk into my life back in Newcastle my dreams of the big smoke and high-heeled journalism began to fade away.

I was still working at G-Star, but also hosting at bars and nightclubs. I was one of those door girls – you know, 'if you're name's not down, you're not coming in' type of people. I'm a little ashamed to admit that I thrived off the power. I went a bit power mad in fact and became such an arsehole. You know, as a student, you're the bottom of the social standing hierarchy, you're drinking doubles for a quid, and you're not exactly glam, are you? So when I went home and had all of my sister's fancy handbags, and all of my mum's fancy spices, and was able to work in nice clubs, I got comfortable and felt like I was 100 per cent that bitch. And it wasn't long before I started going out with an old boyfriend . . . (always, ALWAYS a recipe for disaster, by the way).

So, before I knew it, I'd been back in Newcastle for six months, and the Carrie Bradshaw version of me was a very distant memory. I felt trapped. I wasn't miserable – in fact I thought I was the coolest cat in town – but my world had become really small again. I'd always wanted to travel and live in loads of different places, and have adventures, but I changed during this time and became really happy with this comfortable, reduced world. I'd been out of my comfort zone for so long at uni, and I regressed once I was back in the family home.

Despite this, I don't regret that time – it's when I made all of the amazing friends that I have today. It's when I cemented my incredible relationship with my sister. It's when I got loads of fabulous G-Star jeans. And it was nice to feel safe for a while, after I'd been under so much pressure at uni. But I do remember it being the time in my life when I had the least ambition. I could go out every night of the week. I knew all the doormen in Newcastle. I didn't have to queue anywhere. I never paid for a drink ... and I remember thinking, *life doesn't get any better than this.* Sad cow.

## Daiquiri divas and late-night whistle blowing

This was the stagnant mindset I was in when *Geordie Shore* appeared on my horizon in 2011. I was happy but painfully aware my mates had started to get good jobs, and it was starting to make me feel a bit left behind. There were suddenly fewer people to go out with midweek and I felt this fear that people were starting to move on – everyone, apart from me. It was at this time that MTV were sending groups of young people – undercover producers – out in the nightclubs, asking them to try and spot who would make a good television star. I ran VIP rooms in different bars and nightclubs four nights a week at this point, so chances were they were going to run into me sooner rather than later. Newcastle is a small place, and news travels fast, so I knew who these people were and I'd always look after them, get them a table and a cheap bottle of vodka. I became their unofficial Newcastle tour guide.

I'd be their first port of call when they wanted someone's opinion about anything local. They'd point out
lads and I'd fill them in, 'He talks a good talk, but he
cannot pull a muscle,' and lasses, 'Aww yeah, she'll be
class, she goes over like a granny on ice skates.' And it
grew from there, we built up this really great rapport,
and I still speak to some of them today – despite all the
tears and tantrums, and me probably calling them all
sorts when we were filming drunk and belligerent. We
bonded and I was interested in appearing on the show.
Me and my mates were always out; it was part of the
lifestyle I had then, and I knew we were a laugh and
I was a bit of a character. But I didn't know if MTV
would feel the same way. That all changed one night.
On this occasion, one of the young male producers
was out on his own, looking for big characters, and I
spotted him as me and my mates were booming into
the VIP section of Riverside nightclub.

'You out on your own, mate? I know you're
working, but to everyone here it looks like you're a
creep – why don't you come and stand with us?'

I grabbed him and brought him over to my table
with my pals. Now, I'm a bit of an entertainer when
I've had a drink – or at least I think I am and I love
a fresh audience, so I'm telling this fella this story
and my arms are flying everywhere, and I'm flap-
ping about, and he's laughing, and I'm loving it, and
I'm thriving, so I'm getting even more animated ...

until with my Mr Tickle arms I knock a strawberry daiquiri all over this woman on the table next to us.

Then all hell breaks loose. She starts up, 'You've fucking thrown a drink at me!' Now by this time, I've been working in bars for years. I was selling shots in Liverpool, I'd done a stint in Ibiza, I'd hosted VIP rooms at every nightclub in Newcastle, and I knew how to really handle myself. I wasn't scared of anything – there it was, that silly, ignorant, youthful naivety again. I was fearless.

'I didn't throw a drink at you, I'm so sorry, but you have to calm down.' I tried to explain but she wasn't having any of it, and all her mates were getting in on it too, piping up like a pack of yappy chihuahuas. And I could just see what this was barrelling towards.

Then my mates jumped in. 'Vicky, you can't take this! Don't let her talk to you like that.'

Argh … it was escalating! Everyone's shouting, throwing insults back and forth, two warring tribes of Geordie women, and this little producer is so out of his comfort zone, completely terrified, begging me to leave, and obviously I'm half trying to impress him and I don't want to come across as a raving lunatic, so I agree we should leave, and I gather my girls up. But as we're heading for the door, the daiquiri woman shouts, 'Yeah that's right, walk away, you fucking slag.'

Well, I can't let it go now, can I? Everyone's watching and she's really mugged me off.

I turn around slowly. 'You know what,' I reply, 'I didn't throw that drink at you, it was an accident, because if I had thrown my drink at you, I'd have done it like this.' And I took her drink out of her hand and I threw it right in her face. And it felt good for a split second before I shit myself and screamed, '*Rrruuuuuuuunnnnnnnnn!*' The doormen had heard the ruckus and started to storm in, so fifteen Geordie girls and this one random producer absolutely legged it. Out the back, down the fire exit, away along the quayside, most of us in stilettos, laughing all the way, until we dived into a bunch of waiting cabs at the taxi rank. Phew! We'd escaped the angry doorman and the furious daiquiri-soaked woman, and we were driven to a massive gay club called Powerhouse, where we danced it all off, forgetting all about the argument and just having a right good knees-up. By this time we've all got whistles, we've got pink glittery cowboy hats on, we're doing shots with topless hosts and then we're in the DJ box, all with this little fella who can't believe his night, having the time of his life. He's never had a night out like this, although it was standard practice for me and my mates at this point in our lives.

It got to 5 a.m., and he could barely stand and I knew he had work the next day, so I said, 'Come on, we'll take you back to your hotel,' because I knew he was staying at The Jury's Inn. Me and my mates had him propped up under our shoulders practically carrying him down the corridor, then popped him into his room, and just as we're saying goodbye, he turns to me and says, 'Vicky, don't audition for *Geordie Shore*, don't meet the producers, don't even screen test, just be on the fucking show!'

'If you mean that, call me in the morning,' I said.

And he called me in the morning, and that was that.

## A Shore thing

To be honest, the show was a very difficult time for me, and I was not the best version of myself. I get so much stick for referring to it like that, but here I go again, because I really want to totally clear the air. There's a lot of confusion when it comes to how I feel about *Geordie Shore*, and the record needs to be set straight. I'm eternally grateful to the show and for the platform it has given me. I'm not naïve or arrogant enough to think I'd have got to where I am now, as fast as I have, without it. Mark my words, I was going to get somewhere, but it wouldn't have been so quickly.

However, and it's a big *however*, I was woefully unprepared for what I let myself in for, and I suffered huge ramifications from being so underprepared. I struggled with my mental health, developed an unhealthy dependence on alcohol, had truly toxic relationships, and had a really, really low sense of self-worth. Yes, on the outside looking in we were a bunch of silly young people kissing each other, drinking too much and falling over in bars, but there was more to it than that. What the audience didn't see was the constant pressure I felt I was under to be this incredibly loud, opinionated version of me, because that's what the viewers wanted. I had to be feisty, and swear, and give one-liners, and get drunk and say things I didn't mean, take on everyone I met and stand up to the boys. And being that person all the time, it was draining. Especially when you're in your early twenties and you still haven't worked out if that's who you really are.

Living with eight or nine other people who all have equally strong personalities is a disaster waiting to happen, especially when you throw alcohol and egos into the mix. It made for great television, of course, but I was starting to get bullied on social media and cruel stories were appearing about me in the press. Our fame was in its infancy, and it was a difficult thing to navigate, and we weren't given the best tools. We had a media training day (basically 'say this, don't say that') with two of the 3am Girls from the *Mirror* and that was it. MTV always said they were there for us, and I'm not going to give a scathing indictment of MTV or reality shows in general, but I will say that if I ever have a daughter I would hate her to feel the way I felt. There were many moments that it was made known to me that I was 100 per cent replaceable, not special, and if I didn't march to the beat of their drum the show would happen without me.

This led to the very darkest moments of my life. I was in a really unhealthy relationship, which was a lot worse behind the scenes than people saw on screen. Out of misguided loyalty, I did my best to protect him and hide what was going on, which I know a lot of abuse victims do, but his behaviour was uncovered and he was asked to leave the show. On top of all this, we'd just filmed a series in Australia and I was exhausted and emotionally drained. I really needed some quiet time with my friends and family, time just to be me, because you can't truly be yourself when you're on one of those shows. I was this tiring, switched-on, showbiz version of me. I booked a holiday with friends because I was told we would be given time off to rest and recuperate, the thought of which felt like a lifeline back to mental and physical health. Then, out of nowhere, another series was scheduled. The news was like a punch to the gut. The show was proving so popular and the demand for it was so high, that we had to keep producing more series, but this meant our time off when we could get back to normality was becoming shorter and shorter.

I felt really confused and I knew I was upsetting

my mam. She's since told me that she'd dread the six weeks before I went back into filming a new series because she'd lose her smart, funny, kind daughter, and in her place get a defensive, edgy and frustrated stranger. I was those things because that's how I felt. I was constantly being portrayed as someone I knew I wasn't, and it led me to feel resentful and nervous, and like I couldn't trust anyone.

## Losing control

For someone like me who is a control freak, *Geordie Shore*, or *Ex on the Beach* or *Big Brother*, or any reality show really where you have to totally relinquish your right to have control over your life, is pretty much the scariest thing you can imagine. You have zero say over any situation. Your phone is taken off you. You're told where to go and when. If you're filming you even have to ask for permission to go for a wee. It's not a healthy place for someone to be in for so long, in my opinion, and I did it for five years, from the age of twenty-two until I was twenty-seven. Those years are a turbulent time of anyone's life – figuring out who you want to be and what you want to do, and making some mistakes along the way. But most people don't make mistakes like having sex on television in front of so many people. I'm all up for making mistakes, but it's hard when you wake up in the morning and you don't just have to send a broadcast message to all your pals that reads 'Oh my god, I was so drunk last night and I'm so sorry.' You can't send a blast message to millions of people in sixty-five countries who have seen you kiss your mate's fella, or call everyone a bellend. It's awful. I was really troubled, lost and conflicted.

I was struggling with my identity, and my relationship with my mother deteriorated further. I had been through a horrific break-up, and I needed to rest. I asked for some time off, and the people at the show effectively said, 'Sure, go on holiday, but we'll replace you.' I was told in no uncertain terms that if I took that pre-planned holiday with my friends there would be no place for me on *Geordie Shore* any longer. Now, I knew at this point that it was doing me no favours in regards to my mental health or the public's perception of me, but my confidence was so low and I was so lost that I honestly thought there was nothing else out there for me outside of that show.

I went back in that series, but lost my head. I wasn't mentally strong enough to be there. I knew I was on the verge of a breakdown, and that's when I made one of the biggest mistakes of my life. I had a fight with a girl in a nightclub and I hurt her. It's just so horrible, because I knew something was coming, I knew I was going to break, but it felt like no one around me cared enough to stop me crashing. Of course, my mam loved me, but I was cutting her and the rest of the people who genuinely cared about me out of my life because they wanted me to leave the show, and I was convinced that in order to be successful I had to stay on the show. MTV and my agents at the time convinced me this was true – although I know the decision to continue the show ultimately lay with me. I lashed out. I really hurt her. There was this long, horrible drawn-out court case, again which I deserved but it was nonetheless so horrific. I was described as a monster, as an animal, and I was a criminal. I was all these things, and I knew I wasn't well. Yes, the show had got me fancy shoes, trips abroad, and I'd met some lovely people, but I knew in this moment I wasn't important.

I contemplated suicide. I was told I was going to go to prison and I knew I couldn't cope with that, and I felt like everyone hated me. Even my mam. She wouldn't have anything to do with me, and she totally distanced herself – couldn't be anywhere near me, and I didn't blame her. I remember thinking I wasn't strong enough to get through this. 'This is just the start,' I thought, 'I've got the court case to get through, paparazzi are hiding outside my house, the police are coming to question me all the time . . . I can't cope.' I was still in the family home, but my mam and dad were away on holiday at the time, on a cruise, which I used to bring up every time I'd had a drink. 'You didn't fucking care! You went on a bloody cruise!' And my mam would reply honestly, 'Vicky, at that time, I just didn't know who you were.'

It was my sister Laura and one of my best friends Natalie who never left my side, who wouldn't leave me alone because they were so worried I was going to do something to hurt myself. Laura had to take two weeks off work because she was so scared I'd do something stupid if I was left on my own for a minute. And I saw their pain, but I just couldn't face life anymore. Even if I didn't go to prison, which was the best I could hope for, I was still in my own personal prison – that animal, that monster – I still had to deal with everyone thinking I was those things. What was left except this horrible version of me? I couldn't see a way out of this vicious and destructive cycle I'd got myself into. I couldn't find the courage to try and be better.

This sounds really cheesy, but I might not be here today without those few good people I had around me who I could talk openly with about my mental health at that time. Their love allowed me to stop focusing on the millions of people who didn't matter, the thousands who wrote horrible stuff about me every day online, the journalists who splashed nasty things about me on their front covers every week. And I somehow shifted to this place of gratitude – for my sister, for Natalie, for this friend of mine Nicky who owned a restaurant, and knowing I needed to escape my house and do something nice, had me in after hours so I could go out for the first time in weeks and not have people staring or pointing at me. It was through the kindness of others, and stopping to take a moment to realise that I wasn't all those awful things people said I was, that stopped me from harming myself. I'd been starting to believe it, and it was becoming a self-fulfilling prophecy. I was angry, I was bitchy, I was feisty, and I was aggressive. If you hear enough times that you are a monster you start to believe it, and you start to give everyone what they expect. But then I watched my sister's heart break with worry over me, and felt the love from really decent friends, and I thought if these wonderful people are so concerned about me, I can't be that bad. Those people saved my life.

## Look for the good people

It's so easy to think the worst of yourself, especially when you're still figuring everything out in your twenties – which was when, for me, my mental health issues really came to a head. We all have that really loud inner critic and we're all so ready to believe we're not good or worthy or deserving. But you must not listen, because when you do, the inner critic gets louder and it starts to manifest. You start to act like the worst version of you. Instead, start seeing yourself through the eyes of the people who love you, those people who care, those people who see the best in you. I realised if those people wanted me to still be here, there must be something in me worth saving – even if I couldn't see it in myself. I decided to stop being that version of me I didn't like. I decided to be better.

It was a long journey. I didn't just wake up one day and decide to quit *Geordie Shore*. I had to do a lot of work getting rid of the negative influences. Believe me, it's not like I was considering taking my own life one week, then woke up and overnight became the Vicky Pattison you see before you now. I just realised I could be better, and be the person my sister Laura and friend Natalie deserved to have in their lives.

Take care of yourself, physically and mentally, please. I truly believe that had I been given the time I needed after filming the series in Australia, if I'd had time to rest and get stronger mentally, to escape and just be me for a while, none of this would have happened. Although I had this imposed break during the court case, it wasn't restful – I was full of anxiety, worried about the future. It wasn't what I needed it to be, and I don't think I started the process of getting better until the fog of all that horror was lifted. The court case lasted around six months, and I was charged with assault and affray, and given 180 hours community service plus a £10,000 fine.

Whatever trajectory I was on, I can see now it was an incredibly scary one, drinking too much to cover my anxiety, shouting to cover up my insecurities. And if that fight hadn't happened I would have continued on this scary, dark path, even though it was destroying me. Gosh, I wish it had never taken place, and I wish I had never hurt anybody, because I will never not be disappointed in myself for that. That fight, and everything that ensued from it, was very, very humbling. I was doing personal appearances in Welsh nightclubs, then my sister would drive me back through the night so I could go straight to a charity shop on Wallsend High Street to do eight hours of community service. My life was a real juxtaposition, and everyone thought I was just going to go back and be okay, but this conflict was making me feel incredibly unsettled. Photoshoot, charity shop, nightclub appearance, charity shop, from one day to the next. It was something I had to experience. I had to know what my future held if I kept on the same path.

## Guilty as charged

I have never forgiven myself for that fight. You can forgive drunken fights with your friends, kissing someone when you shouldn't, cheating on a school test, but you can't forgive yourself for hurting someone, and you can't forget how inflicting that pain on someone made you feel. I can't forget the things that people called me. As a long-term goal, I would love to absolve myself of that guilt but realistically, I don't know if it's possible. That moment was pivotal in my life and made me realise the person I *didn't* want to be. Maybe you've had moments like that, too? The guilt and horror of it nearly made me take my own life. If I forget that event and those feelings it sparked, who knows what I could become again? It's painful but I don't know if the alternative is worth thinking about. I wouldn't be here.

Life is not meant to be easy, but I've since learnt that guilt can be all-consuming. It's okay to make mistakes, especially in your twenties – to me, it's the best way to learn – but you can't let feelings of guilt take over your life like it almost did mine. Try and be more self-compassionate, commit to self-kindness instead of self-blame, and don't beat yourself up when you feel you're messing things up. I think the years between the ages of twenty and thirty are hard for us all, aren't they? You're brave just getting through each day, and it takes courage just to show up sometimes. Be kind. Let go of past regrets. Know yourself so well that you can tell when you're on the cusp of something, bad or good, and take a few brave steps out of your comfort zone to a happier, healthier place, knowing that your courage will be rewarded.

I turned my whole life around; I became someone I was proud to look at in the mirror; I saved my relationships with my good friends and family and I nurture them every day. I've found real pleasure in life. I've lifted myself up. And none of it would have been possible if I hadn't been brave, if I hadn't taken that one step of leaving *Geordie Shore*. And don't think you have to take giant leaps or quick steps, it doesn't have to be either of those things. Just one small step, and then a few more steps, then a few more . . . Every time I kept walking, I got further away from the person I didn't want to be and those people I knew I shouldn't be around, and gradually before I knew it, I was far away, striding – and I don't even recognise that person anymore.

Have faith. If anyone feels as helpless as I found myself at that time in my life, I want you to know you will have bad moments, and bad days, and bad weeks, but they don't last forever. When you're in the thick of despair, it's difficult to believe that. I certainly couldn't believe that at the time! I didn't think I'd ever have a good day again, which is why I thought the best thing to do would be to end my life and stop embarrassing my mam and hurting my sister, and just stop the pain. But, if I had taken my own life, I wouldn't have seen how things could get better, and how I was on the cusp of unlocking all this great potential, and I wouldn't have this incredible life I've got now.

I had the knowledge somewhere deep and buried inside of me that bad times don't last forever. You are not under any obligation to be the same person you were ten years ago, ten months ago, even ten minutes ago. I learnt this, trust this, and at the same time appreciated that I could be happy again. And you can too.

## The Secret To... Surviving the most turbulent time of your life

As I've outlined in the chapter above, you must remember being imperfect is not a sign of weakness – it's a sign you are human. Accept your limits and build a life that works for *you*, not a life you think everyone else wants to see. Talk to yourself how you'd talk to a good friend, and know you can:

* Take a break from the rush and carefully consider what you actually want to achieve. Don't let the panic of your twenties push you into some dark places or bad mental spaces.

* Ask for help if you need it. It might feel like now you're in your twenties you're an adult and should have everything sussed and sorted, but that is rarely the case. Don't be afraid or ashamed to ask for advice from people who you respect.

* Allow yourself a bad day and move on. Don't feel bad about things you've done in the past when you could be focusing that energy on the future.

✳ Say no. Even in your twenties, when you're new to things and looking for opportunities, you don't have to accept anything simply because it's on offer.

✳ Own your pain – I like to say feel your feels – and allow yourself to reflect, feel low, and cry if you have to. There is no point storing up emotions, because they will escape at some point, even if it's when you're old and sorted.

✳ Give yourself a compliment. Acknowledging the stuff you're getting right will help you feel less shit about the stuff you may have got wrong. Everyone deserves a pat on the back sometimes.

✳ Try something new. You are never stuck or trapped, whether you're in your teens, twenties or eighties. You can change careers, move cities, leave behind unhealthy habits for ones that make you feel good. Who you are as a teen or twenty-something does not have to define you or your life forever.

## PREPARE YOUR PURPOSE

Grab a pen and find a quiet place to think, and use the space below to note down the goals you have for the next decade, or even the next week if you can't see that far ahead. Question your motives – will these changes and additions make your life happier? Will they bring kinder, better influences into your life? Jot down the date, and your mood, and keep adding to your list as inspiration comes to you.

What do you want to achieve?

_____

_____

_____

_____

_____

What do you want to let go of?

_____

_____

_____

_____

_____

How will you make this happen?

_____

_____

_____

_____

_____

# 2

# Learning to love the skin you're in

*Life is too short not to order the cake.*
*Eat it, enjoy it, and be kind to yourself.*

I would love to claim that it was simply fame and social media that has affected my self-worth and that gave me a negative body image over the years, but these things were, unfortunately, an issue I was always going to have. I'm sure many of you, sadly, have had similar issues over the years, or still have now. I was a tiny baby; 5 pounds 11 ounces and weirdly really, really long. I shot out of my mam, and my dad took one look at me and said I looked like a skinned rabbit. My father, ladies and gentlemen! Always complimentary. I joke, but from a very young age, I have always had issues around my body and what other people thought of it.

Anyone who knows me, follows me on Instagram, watched me on *Celebrity MasterChef,* or has ever had the misfortune of seeing me in a restaurant (I swear every time it's like that scene from *When Harry Met Sally* – you know the one) will know how much I love my food. I'm a total piglet! I honestly believe that carbs are my one true love. This relationship has been a lifelong love affair, so it didn't take long before I left my skinned-rabbit phase behind and embraced pure childhood chunk. Like most kids, I got told, 'Finish your plate, some kids aren't lucky enough to have food like you!' My grandma was a big feeder and I loved the bones of her – Grandma Mavis was one of the strongest female influences in my life, so I always finished my plate. I see kids these days moaning, 'I don't like this' or 'I don't like that', and my grandma or mam wouldn't have had that. I knew I had to eat everything put in front of me, which was never a problem.

But it was difficult being a chubby kid. Really early on, as soon as I started going to school, I was aware that my friends were smaller, slimmer, daintier. I was the big girl. I'm curvy now so it makes sense I was always going to have a bit of puppy fat. I didn't mind that to a painful degree until I got older, when I started to notice that my body shape was unrepresented, and that I wasn't as conventionally pretty or attractive as the other girls. Let's face it, there weren't any bigger girls in the Spice Girls. When everyone was fighting in the playground over who got to be

Posh Spice or Baby Spice, I always had to pretend to be whichever one was left over. 'You can't be Baby, she wears a belly top,' I still remember school friends telling me as a pre-teen. If I could, I'd love to go back in time and tell those twig bitches that Pooh Bear wore a belly top and absolutely rocked it, but back then, I didn't have the confidence. (FYI, Pooh Bear is a body positivity icon and should be respected as such.)

## The weight of womanhood

It must be something that's in us girls, and I don't know whether our mothers had to deal with it when they were children too, but I imagine they did. No shade to the mothers or fathers that raised my generation, but I don't think they were as educated about the ramifications of not embracing different body shapes, and being kind to others, as parents raising little girls are today. It's a movement just taking off now. When I was young, kids didn't know that they should be accepting of different shapes and sizes because there were no girls that looked like me on television or in the magazines – all the women on *Friends* were super skinny and I think, in the back of my mind when I was a child, I just assumed I'd grow up to look like them. I'd get taller, my weight would fall off, and I'd even out into one, gorgeous, Rachel-like package. But of course, it doesn't happen like that.

I grew up and, as a teenager, my body changed. I got into sports and the puppy fat turned to muscle. I got strong . . . but not smaller. I looked athletic, and that body felt better to live in. I felt more capable, less vulnerable, and that has been a mentality that has stayed with me ever since. Even today, when I train hard and feel physically fit, I feel mentally capable of a lot more, thanks to the endorphin boost. I'm sure it harks back to that moment when I stopped being an insecure, chubby pre-teen and became a more confident woman in my late teens. I enjoyed that change; I felt more able to look after myself.

However, this acceptance of my body didn't last long and any feelings I had about my body were exacerbated when I landed in the public eye. Having other people negatively point out things about your body that you're *already* worried about is savage; you're never going to be able to take it on the chin, especially in your early twenties when you're proper struggling with your identity, self-image and body acceptance in general. When we first started doing *Geordie Shore*, I remember feeling like we didn't quite fit in. At the time, there were three big reality TV shows on the scene – *Geordie Shore*, *The Only Way Is Essex* and *Made in Chelsea* – and we were all constantly being compared to one another in the press, even though we were all really different. But it didn't matter, and it felt like we never came out on top. The girls from *The Only Way Is Essex* were really glamorous, always had a full face of makeup, always looked so perfect, and all the boys really fancied them because they only had a couple of glasses of prosecco on a night out and didn't fall out of nightclubs shouting, swearing and demanding kebabs. The girls from *Made in Chelsea* were all ludicrously skinny and super cosmopolitan, and probably all had houses in the south of France and daddies who owned half of Buckinghamshire. We were from different worlds in every conceivable way, but all of the comparisons between us still came flooding in and I remember feeling I didn't quite measure up in the world I'd found myself in. That's when my real trouble with body image started. I felt incurably insecure, really inferior, intimidated and just so ugly.

My self-worth was at an all-time low. In 2011, when I was twenty-three, I remember doing a *Nuts* magazine photoshoot that I didn't want to be in in the first place because my mam was fuming. 'First the reality television show, and now a lads' mag? When is it going to stop?' she said. 'Well, I hope they're paying you well at least.' I told her I wouldn't be getting my boobs out, and that I'd just be in my underwear, but I felt conflicted. I went ahead because the pressure from MTV, and the rest of the girls in the cast, was ridiculous – because if I didn't do it, *Nuts* didn't want any of them. It was an all-or-nothing package. It had been a dream of Holly's at the time, and I remember feeling if I didn't do it I'd be letting everyone down. And I was already getting a bit of a reputation as the 'boring one'. So I did it.

To be clear: I don't regret doing the photoshoot, or any of the sexy shoots I've done since. That first shoot was tough, though. I was so nervous, a fish out of water and not a model, and I didn't know how to pose. At that early point in my career, I was still sticking my thumb up in all my pictures. I did finally get into the swing of things and it wasn't degrading at all, I felt empowered – it was my body and I could do what I wanted with it. I had a lacy leotard type thing on, and the photographer said I was doing great and he'd definitely have me back again, and I was getting dead into it. But then I went to get changed into my next outfit, and was chatting to the stylist. 'You look really good, I don't know why you were so nervous,' she said. I told her it was because I was tired because we'd just finished filming a series, and I'd drunk so much I didn't feel in great condition, and she replied, 'Once you lose a little bit of weight, you'll be fine.'

She probably didn't even mean to make me feel rubbish, or maybe she did, but whatever the reason was, I just shrank. I went from feeling like William Large Penis, and being so proud of myself for getting out of my comfort zone and trying something new, to just feeling so small and pathetic. In one fell swoop that woman had reduced me to nothing more than a clothes size and all of my old insecurities came tumbling back. Instantly I felt fat, and not attractive enough, and wondered why any man would want to look at a photo of me in a magazine. I remember feeling like I had to accept everyone else's opinion about my body and that they had a right to say anything they wanted about it. And honestly, all the cruel comments, the negativity, the jibes, everything people said to me – it was nothing new, nothing I hadn't already said to myself and been saying to myself for years. It was just horrible knowing that the worst things you thought about yourself, other people thought too. It was hard to deal with on so many levels, and it made me start to truly hate myself.

## Out of control

I felt painfully out of control in this new world I was in. I was on a show that by its very nature took away every inch of my independence. It was a juggernaut and I was taken along for the ride. I felt like I was losing even more of myself, and my weight suddenly became the only aspect of my life I thought I could control. I couldn't control how they edited me, or showed me, and I couldn't control what Charlotte or Gary said about me in green-screen filming. Neither could I control what Brenda from Barnsley wrote about me on Twitter or how Dave from Darlington hated the very bones of me. What I *could* control was what I put in my mouth. And it became an obsession. It wasn't just about what I was eating – it was how I was exercising, and how I was treating my body, and it came to a head after that court case in 2014, when I was feeling suicidal. I was so out of control, I felt like I had no say over my future, I felt I had to take on the chin whatever people decided about me, and I lost it. I lost my head. I can't say I starved myself, because I'm too greedy, but I didn't eat enough for a person my size. I'm five foot six and I was limiting myself to 1000 calories per day. Nowadays, I can wallop that in one meal. If you're in a hurry and you grab yourself a sandwich, a packet of crisps and a chocolate bar – you're done, job's a good'un! On top of limiting my calories I was also exercising obsessively, twice a day, weights in the morning, cardio at night. Please know that as I write this, I'm not having a go at people who are super motivated to exercise. I still love training, but I was doing it for all the wrong reasons. I wasn't doing it to be healthy and strong or as a mood eleva-tor, I wasn't doing it because I knew I'd feel powerful and capable afterwards. I was doing it because I needed to see that number come down on the scales, and if it didn't, I knew I'd have to eat less the next day. There was nothing positive about it; it was all about control and fear and hating myself. I convinced myself it wasn't that, and it's only been in the last couple of years that I've seen it. I had disordered eating.

With this mindset I was never going to be thin enough, I was never going to have trained enough, and it was draining trying to keep up with these unattainable and unrealistic goals I was trying to reach. It stole so much of my youth. I know I'm going on like I'm Grandmother Willow (you know, the old tree from Disney's *Pocahontas*?). But honestly, I wish I could get back some of my twenties. It looked to everyone else, I'm sure, like I was having so much fun – and fuck me, I was at times – and I'm not being all 'woe is me', but if I could have had just an ounce of the self-acceptance I have now in my thirties, I'd have been so much happier. I was constantly wrapped up in my insecurities and self-doubt, paired with a crippling desire to look a certain way which was so futile and pointless. I missed out on so much enjoyment and contentment, and that is a real shame. I'm sure I'm not alone.

## Not so sexy six

So, you think you're going to get to this goal weight, and this goal size – which for me then was size 6 – and you're going to look in the mirror and love what you see. The problem is, it's never going to be enough. When your self-worth hinges on a number, even when you see that number staring back at you, it's never going to be low enough, and your thighs are never going to be small enough, and your bones are never going to be prominent enough. I remember being in Essex, in a size 6 skirt from River Island, for a birthday night out, and shouting around to my mates, 'I just can't find anything smaller!' as this skirt was hanging off me. I was so proud of that. But it was the head-space I'd gotten myself into, a toxic mentality. There was never a moment when I looked at myself and said, 'You've smashed this, Vic, you look lovely!' I'd always just go straight to the negative, tell myself, 'Your thighs still do look quite big.'

It was around this time, in 2013, that I recorded my fitness DVD. I was obsessed with fitness, just for the wrong reasons. There are so many positives to being fit and healthy, I had just grown up and was surrounded with conflicting messages about what body positivity really was and what it looked like. I wanted to believe all the things I was saying in my DVD. Get fit, get healthy, get toned with me! Learn to love yourself. But it took longer for my mind to get there, to let go of this one version of being perfect that I'd been fed since I was young. Obviously, people could now say to me the fitness DVD I recorded before I accepted my imperfections were a scam, but it wasn't a sham at the time and I believed everything I was saying. I never misled anyone on purpose. In ten years' time, I might be sitting somewhere, saying that this version of me that I'm projecting right now isn't right either; we all change and grow. I just want to note here, for the record, that I never set out to fool anybody, or trick anybody, when I recorded those DVDs. I was totally invested in what I was saying and truly believed that being the skinniest version of me possible would make me happy.

I fought with that size 6 woman for a few years, that eight-stone giant bobblehead I had become, but what ultimately took over was my desire to live. For me, when I look back at any of the pivotal moments in my life, it's when I get to the brink of total devastation that I stop and take stock. The one thing that saves me from going too far every time is that I want to live. I really do, and I don't mean a half-life, some painfully fake existence when I don't like who I am, where I'm constantly scared, where I won't eat the fucking cheeseboard or have a glass of wine. I mean a life full of friends and laughter, and colour and carbs! What stopped me from being this size 6 dicky-bird of a woman for the rest of my life was that I missed having fun. I missed drinking WKDs. I wanted to roll home from a night with my girls, grabbing a Domino's pizza on the way. I wanted to sit and hug my boyfriend on the sofa and order in a Chinese takeaway. I wanted to travel to new places and eat paella in the sunshine. That's the only life I wanted. A life with passion, waking up excited and having fire in your belly and literal food, for fuck's sake. That's what stopped my dangerous obsession: I wanted to be happy and being a size 6 made me miserable. I wanted a healthy, balanced life full of fun more than I wanted to be a size 6.

You know still, today, whenever I share a post on social media of me enjoying a nice meal, or having a treat, there's always one woman who comments, 'You're always eating, how do you stay so slim?' or 'Gosh, you love your food!' And I know it doesn't come from a bad place, but it's this ideology that's been drummed into all of us that if you want to be healthy and happy, or attractive, you cannot enjoy your food. I spent so many years, all of my adult life practically, not ordering what I wanted in a restaurant, sitting scouring the pdf of the menu the night before I went out, looking for the lowest calorie item, which more often than not was a fucking Caesar salad without the croutons, without the dressing – without anything that makes it nice, quite frankly. I spent years chucking away £20 for a bag of iceberg lettuce and a bit of dried-up chicken breast, which was painful on every level.

## Finally finding freedom

How did I find balance? And how can you, if you're struggling in a similar way with your body image like I was? First of all, chuck out your scales. Scales have no place in anyone's home. I know there will be personal trainers reading this thinking I'm wrong, but how dare we let a tiny piece of battery-operated technology control our entire mood? If you're going to let any tiny piece of battery-operated technology control your mood, it best be your vibrator! I know this might sound daunting to some of you, but please think about it: why does your weight have to be so intrinsically linked to your self-worth? Go by how you feel in your head instead, or how you feel in your clothes. This journey to accepting your natural body shape is slow and at times difficult – it was for me. I unequivocally know by now that being super skinny and having disordered eating did not bring me happiness – I wasn't smug when I got to my dream size, I didn't think I always looked great, or that no one could ever take a bad picture of me again. For a while, in fact, I actually went the other way and became even more critical of myself, probably because I was so downright hungry all the time.

I knew by this point that being skinny wasn't the answer to my happiness. I missed my friends, I wasn't having fun, I was constantly hungry, and constantly controlled by the number on the scale, and it didn't bring me the joy I thought it would – or even help build my self-esteem. But then going the other way didn't either. When I was hungover all the time on *Geordie Shore*, stuffing myself with processed food, eating out every night, I felt sluggish, rubbish and lethargic. Neither end of this spectrum brought me joy or peace and I realised in a great big fucking lightbulb epiphany moment, after years of torturing myself, that happiness had to lie in the middle. Why it took me so long to work this out I don't know, but it did.

It was the years of flip-flopping between starving and stuffing that allowed me to find an even keel and balance out the extremes I'd lived by in the past. When I was in *Geordie Shore*, drinking too much, sometimes five nights a week, and walloping kebabs and nuggets for funsies, I was uncomfortable and unhappy. I wasn't exercising at all in those days. There was no time. It's an incredibly jam-packed day when you're on the old *Geordie Shore*, and people assume you're having a lovely time, but it's graft. And then when I was obsessed with calories, working out and being the thinnest I could be, I had no social life at all. On a night out, I'd allow myself three vodka, lime and sodas, which I can still remember – I had it all worked out – were around eighty calories each, so I could have the three for less than 250 kcals. God forbid a barman came near my drink with some lime cordial. 'No, no, no – fresh lime! Fresh lime!' The amount of bar staff's heads I've bitten off because of lime cordial – you'd have thought they were trying to mainline heroin into my veins the way I carried on! But the thought of that much untracked sugar in my drink had my anxiety through the roof. Becoming obsessed with my diet and exercise led me to feel anxious, never good enough, and constantly dreaming of the day I would be thinner, never feeling any contentment with the body I was living in. Yes, it was nice for a little bit of time to know I could walk into any shop and look good in absolutely anything, but what's the point of knowing you'll look good in absolutely anything if you're going absolutely nowhere? Even if you did feel like you looked good when you were smaller, what's the point of even going out if you're so fucking worried all the time it turns you into a total wet lettuce?

I remember once, during this period of my life, I had a trip to the cinema planned and instead of being excited and thinking, *oh, I love Leonardo DiCaprio*, I was worried about the popcorn, frantically working out that a large box was roughly 660 calories, and if I ate it, I'd only have 340 calories to play with for the rest of the day. That's how my mind used to work.

It made me realise neither of those extremes were good for me and slowly – because it was a slow progression to the happy, healthy spot I'm in right now – I knew the middle ground was where I needed to be. I got so sick of punishing myself for having the body that was given to me. A bit of this self-awareness comes with getting older and growing up a bit too; you realise there's more to life than seeing a particular number pop up on a scale. It becomes clearer that it's more important to have fun with family, and be a great pal, and be a cool girlfriend, than being a size 6 or a size 8. So much of life is socialising and creating memories with people you love, and forging fun times as you build relationships, which is harder to do when you can't think about anything else other than getting to the gym or the calorie content of a Twix.

## The pressure to be perfect

Everyone deals with the pressure to look a certain way. Yes, being in the limelight exacerbated it, but we're all faced daily with these constant images of perfection, bombarded with them on television, and in magazines, and on social media – we're always being reminded that we don't measure up, and being told we could be better, that someone else is doing it effortlessly while working as hard as you. You have no excuses. It feels in a way like people – and women especially – are being kept down, to doubt ourselves because that makes us weaker. We need to stop consuming this rubbish the patriarchy is feeding us if we want to stop feeling like this.

There was a definitive moment for me at the end of 2018, and although at the time it was really hard, it got my head in the right space. I had a run of three really heartbreaking events: I lost my best friend suddenly; my relationship broke down after I was cheated on publicly; and my grandma Mavis passed away. I found myself at a real loss as to how to cope. I think any of those events would have been enough to take the wind out of anybody's sails, but the three together left me facing a breakdown. Everyone was watching what I was going to do next, especially after my ex cheated, and I just had no energy anymore. I was fighting off grief and felt so drained that just putting my clothes on each morning and placing one foot in front of the other was taking everything I had.

And in that state, I no longer had the energy to project an image of perfection out into the world, something I'd been trying to do for years – an image that proved I was strong, together, unfazed by anything life threw at me. Brave, beautiful, glamorous, powerful, all these things that women are told we need to be all the fucking time – plus emotionally stable – I mean heaven forbid you shed a tear in public! I could not do it anymore, and honesty just poured out of me. I no longer had it in me to keep up a façade about anything. I started putting it all out there, warts and all, through sheer accident ... and it's the best thing I ever did for myself, and the best thing, I hope, I've ever given to other people.


## Behind the mask

The veil of perceived perfection fell on the floor, and the true world of crazy that is the life of Vicky Pattison with her bloated belly, her spotty face, her wild emotions – all of it came out. And I am now so comfortable being myself. When you do that, when you present yourself unfiltered, you in turn inspire other people to do the same, and you give the other people in your life permission to do the same, to properly embrace who they are, and shine for who they are. We can help each other sparkle! My followers know that when they come onto my Instagram, I won't make them feel guilty or lesser if they haven't smashed all their goals that day, or ticked off everything on their to-do list, or have a full face of makeup on. No, you guys can check my profile and see that I haven't brushed my hair that morning. And too right! We put too much pressure on ourselves, and when I stopped trying to be perfect, because I had no energy, and that authentic, organic version of me was revealed, that was when great reactions started.

One of my favourite reactions was from Susannah Constantine when I was in the jungle. She said to me, 'You know before I got in here and got to know you, I'd have hated my daughter to see how you behaved on *Geordie Shore* and thought that was acceptable. But now I've met you, I would love nothing more than for my daughter to grow up and be like you.' It was so lovely, because that's all I ever wanted to do when I went into the jungle; to show people that there was more to me than the hard-partying, big-drinking foghorn they'd come to know. So, when I share my honest moments, and my squishy bits, and my bad angles, and all the rest of it – when women say I'm going to show my daughter this, or I've told my daughter to follow you, that really resonates with me, because when I was young, I didn't have anyone telling me that there was more than one way to be beautiful. I didn't have anyone telling me even if you haven't got a washboard stomach popping out from under a crop top, you're still worthy and wonderful.

I want young girls to know that there is not one way to be beautiful, and it is not all hinged on your physical appearance. It's about how you make other people feel, your work ethic, your sense of humour, how you treat people you interact with on a daily basis. How you look is such a small part of your identity. You should be proud of your so-called flaws, because they make you who you are, and perfect doesn't exist.

So, when people see what I'm doing and talk about their daughters it makes me well up with tears every time – and I just want you to know, if you're reading this, and you have posted something like that on my Instagram, I have read it and cried.

## Hope wins

I feel positive for the future. I feel young girls – and young people of any gender, for that matter – are going to grow up and not be so scared. I have every faith that women have had enough of this bullshit, of being diminished, and we're done with being told we have to be smaller to be attractive, we are done with being shrunk. We want to take over in every sense of the word. We want to dominate, smash our goals, and be incredible powerhouse women, and I believe there are so many of these women blazing a trail – whether it's sharing it all on their Instagram account, being the Vice President of the United States of America, or whether it's being a mother. Whatever your goals are, you're doing it, you're killing it. And like me, I know you're fucking sick of being told how we should be or what we should want. Yes, this body positivity movement has legs – and it's going to grow, and grow and grow! Because it's about time we collectively took control of every aspect of our lives, including our bodies and our image. Finding self-love and loving your body is not an easy journey, but we can find inner strength when we look out for one another, and start to deconstruct the societal standards that have made us feel shit about ourselves – unnecessarily – for so long.

## Face value

I've had longer to come to terms with body positivity, but I'll hold my hand up and admit that the ageing thing is something new to me and it's something I continue to struggle with. I think a lot of that has to do with the times we're living in. I feel a lot of things exploded at once – reality television, social media and readily available cosmetic surgery. All three burst onto the scene at the same time and they feed off each other and people's insecurities about how they should look – and I mean everyone, not just those in the public eye.

I've witnessed first hand what can happen when you don't love who you are and you're not okay with just being yourself. I'm not going to name names or point fingers, because it's everyone's individual choice how they choose to look and how they choose to represent themselves, and everyone's journey is different and I'm not a judgemental person, *but* I made a conscious decision when I was about twenty-seven years old to *not* do anything to my face. I was surrounded by a lot of people who were full of fillers and Botox, and doing a lot of stuff when their faces were still forming, and I couldn't get my head round it. I've struggled with my body image, my skin and my self-worth but I've always been okay with my face. My lips always looked normal, although of course now they look small compared to everyone else's. I've got nice green eyes. I didn't want to end up looking in a mirror and not see me staring back. I see people now who I used to know and they don't look like themselves anymore, and it's a shame because I know I'm not always proud of everything I do, and I have made fashion and makeup mistakes, and have had hairdos I'd rather forget, but it's all part of the fun and doesn't have to last longer than a night out. Things that are more permanent scare me – partly because I'm a total fanny but also partly because I'm so fickle. I can LOVE an outfit one day and not be able to stand the sight of it the next. So, imagine if I was making huge changes to my face? I'd constantly just be in turmoil. No, it's not for this fickle fanny, fortunately. (That was fun to say, wasn't it?)

So I took this quite aggressive stance against the things people were injecting into their face when I was on the right side of thirty. But now that I'm past thirty-three, I have some days when I think, *shit, you've really backed yourself into a corner here, haven't you Pattison!* I know I'm allowed to change my mind, but I kind of don't want to. I can't tell women, young lasses, or anyone anywhere that they are beautiful just as they are when I'm desperately trying to change who I am. It's horrible that we're pressurised to feel like we have to. Some days I wake up and I think, *you're doing all right for thirty-three, kiddo*, and some days I don't. And I have things that help with that. I might have taken a stand against Botox, but I love a fancy facial, I'm forever asking all my makeup artists I meet for their top tips, and buying creams and potions. SPF – every day, I swear by it. I love to treat myself to self-care. I love to have a nice spa day. I drink plenty of water and I love green tea so I drink lots of that. And I eat plenty of vegetables. This all helps my skin feel plump and hydrated. I'm kind of doing more to ward off wrinkles from the inside than the outside right now.

There's plenty of ways to look after yourself, and feel good and feel fresh, without injecting anything into your face. I've talked to loads of people about this subject, and how you look on the outside is about what is happening on the inside. So, do remember that! And be kind to yourself. A huge part of life is changing and growing up. Some days I'll look on Instagram and I think, *how the fuck am I the only person on here getting older?* I just sit and stare, looking at other people's profiles, and say, 'I know you're older than me so how do you look younger than me? Why do I look like I could be your mother?' I sometimes get so frustrated but I have to tell myself that I've lived, I've had boyfriends, I've been to different countries, I've got a degree, I've made amazing TV shows and met amazing people, I've made some great big mistakes and some terrible small decisions, I've experienced things in life I never thought I would ... and that all shows on your face. I can't look twenty-one years old and have all those memories. I'm growing old somewhat disgracefully, and most days I'm okay with that. But I am really working on being okay with it all days – which I suppose, like everything, will just take time.

## My menstrual manifesto

I grew up in a house that wasn't exactly period proud, which is nothing against my mam – that's a genuine reflection of the time. Women were ashamed of their periods, and periods scared men, so if you talked about them, you did so with a stiff upper lip, or you just pulled on your big girl knickers and went to school. It was indoctrinated into me that I couldn't talk about my periods, that they should be hidden because they were shameful – and that stayed with me. *Don't scare blokes by talking about them. Don't be weak by complaining about them.* It's all such negative reinforcement.

The fact we can create life is pretty incredible. Don't get me wrong, I think birth sounds horrific and I think we should all be able to just lay an egg like a chicken and be done with it. I mean, I can't understand why it's the twenty-first century and we can't just lay an egg? I guarantee if blokes had to give birth, we'd all be laying eggs by now. 110 per cent. But as it is women are still enduring sixty-five hours of labour, while men say, 'Awww, it can't be that bad, try getting kicked in the balls.' Dicks. The fact that many of us can create life, give birth, nurse offspring, and keep this world turning is incredible and the idea we are supposed to feel ashamed of how our bodies make this possible doesn't sit well with me.

So, let's just get one thing straight, shall we? As a woman you're not meant to be open about periods, you're not meant to talk about the pain, the debilitating cramps, the clumsiness, the emotional rollercoaster of mood swings that comes with it, not being able to articulate ourselves properly – so many things we're apparently supposed to suffer through in silence. No. I'm sorry, but no. I call bullshit. I'm so done with it. When you don't talk about these things you don't know what is normal or not and that is deeply unhelpful to all of us.

I've been on a bit of a journey with my period. I've

recently removed the implant that I had in my arm for fifteen years (I should add they were various different implants over that time, but always the same form of contraception), and now that I'm talking openly about my periods, I'm annoyed about what I put myself through for so long. Nobody told me there was something else better out there. I assumed everyone bled heavily for seven days, cried solidly for the two weeks beforehand, smashed glasses, and hated their partner with a burning passion that consumed their soul. I convinced myself that this was normal, because the alternative, that it didn't have to be like this and maybe I could talk to someone about it, was a bit embarrassing. Speaking up and saying I needed help would make me weak. Where do we get programmed to think this way? Who made us feel advocating for ourselves made us lesser? We didn't come up with these ideas on our own, I'm sure of it.

I'm not sure I'm ready for children yet so I still need contraception, but I want the right one for me. I need to work out my relationship with my periods, and since I've been open about it on social media, so many wonderful women have come forward with advice, sharing information with me about endometriosis and premenstrual dysphoric disorder. They've come forward with all these amazing, helpful ideas and suggestions that had never occurred to me – and they never occurred to me because I'd never talked to anybody, because I thought I just had to put on a brave face and get on with it. But sharing our collective experiences gives us power. A problem shared truly is a problem halved, and when you open up to people, to warrior women who are going through the same or similar things you are going through, you feel less alone. You feel part of a community, you gain knowledge. You learn things you didn't know. You feel part of something. The more I share the more I want to share, and it's an incredibly liberating feeling.

## The beauty within

We all need self-compassion. For years I beat myself up, telling myself I wasn't beautiful or thin enough, or that it was a problem that I didn't look like everybody else. And you know, I put my body and mind through hell trying to look like everybody else. And when I got to that time when I looked most like other women who I thought I had to emulate, I wasn't happy at all. Being beautiful is about being kind to yourself, giving yourself compassion, finding self-love, and it all starts from within. Having cellulite on your thighs, a breakout on your chin, bingo wings, none of these things define you – they add to your character, they make you human, they make you beautiful in your own unique way. Nobody is perfect. And even these amazing glossy images you see on social media aren't real. They are filtered – and filtered life is not real life.

I'd say redefine your perceived flaws, fixate on the things you do well in life, and be proud of who you are. If we all looked the same it would be really boring. Remember, variety is the spice of life. That's one of my favourite sayings because it's so true. Me and my mates, we all go out and we'll all fancy a different fella or girl and this is perfectly normal. But when it comes to looking at the things that make us different or unique, we see variety as a negative, and only see the worst in ourselves. We all need to stop it. Silence your inner critic and instead of pulling out the things you hate about yourself, dragging yourself down, pick out things you do like. Focus on that and build yourself up. You will achieve so much more, you'll have a smile on your face, you'll have a good day, and in turn your happiness will affect others. They'll have a great day; they'll be kinder to people. Who knows, you might stop a troll from trolling because they feel better about who they are.

Maybe you don't yet know the power of telling yourself you're beautiful. Please upgrade your negative narrative. Be gentle on yourself, even as your body changes – because it will change, as you age, or fight illness, or get pregnant. We're all evolving. Be gentle on your body because it's the only one you've got. Even if sometimes it's hard to love, it is your home and deserves your respect. Stop beating yourself up. Some days you will be bigger, some days you will be smaller; some days your stomach will feel flatter, some days your thighs will feel wobblier. None of this defines your self-worth. What defines your self-worth is how you're making memories and how you're making people feel, what you're achieving and how you're achieving it. These things make you *you*, not whether you're a size 6 in a River Island skirt or not. Accept yourself and let go of any toxic narratives that make you believe shrinking yourself in any way will lead to happiness. Be proud to burn bright, shine like the star you are and in turn encourage those around you to be larger than life and beautiful in every conceivable way.

# *The Secret To… loving the skin you're in*

Rather than fixating on things you don't like about your physical appearance, nurture your body *and* mind with self-care and positivity. Think, how much better would you feel if you woke up each morning and just loved yourself? It'll be easy to:

* Listen to your physical needs, your body will always tell you what you want – whether it's a bloody vegetable once in a while, goddammit Vicky, or a rest. Listen to it;

* Appreciate your body – it is your home and it has gotten you this far, so be kind to it;

* Know your worth, inside and out – you are beautiful, strong and powerful beyond measure and it's about time you realised it. Try telling yourself that every morning, or come up with your own positive affirmations. You can say anything you want, but just make sure you're getting up and taking control of your day and how you see yourself;

* Celebrate your wins, workouts and good choices. Give yourself a pat on the back when you pick

the green juice over the bacon sandwich because you've had a big weekend and you know it's what your body is crying out for. That is a power move and deserves your acknowledgement.

* Accept your changes, free of fear. Your body will be different at different points in your life. Relax, this is natural and shape or size doesn't define you. Your attitude to change does. So go forward with sass and grace and be 100 per cent that bitch regardless of your dress size.

* Set yourself healthy boundaries and goals – don't be afraid to put yourself first and also always be realistic.

* Support other women through their moments of self-doubt. Girls compete with each other; strong women empower other women. Don't ever forget that.

* . . . Oh, and always, ALWAYS order the fucking chips.

## PREPARE YOUR PURPOSE

Change how you talk to yourself when you look in the mirror. Recognise negative self-talk for what it is: harmful, pointless and untrue. Instead of checking out your reflection and thinking *I'm not good enough, I'm too fat, my skin is terrible,* find things about your appearance that you do like, or repeat positive mantras that will boost instead of diminish your confidence. Tell yourself you have good skin, pretty eyes, cute dimples or a magnetic personality. Stop being your own worst critic, give yourself a wink in the mirror, and know that the beauty inside you shines through. Use the lines on the next page to note down the negative self-talk you're practising at the moment, and alongside it write down the things you know you should be saying instead – and will say in the future. For example, replace 'I have a big bum' with 'I have an ass that just won't quit.' Re-read the list when you need a solid reminder of your own love language!

| Negative self-talk | What I should say instead |
| --- | --- |
| _____ | _____ |
| _____ | _____ |
| _____ | _____ |
| _____ | _____ |
| _____ | _____ |
| _____ | _____ |
| _____ | _____ |
| _____ | _____ |
| _____ | _____ |
| _____ | _____ |
| _____ | _____ |
| _____ | _____ |

| Negative self-talk | What I should say instead |
|---|---|
| _____ | _____ |
| _____ | _____ |
| _____ | _____ |
| _____ | _____ |
| _____ | _____ |
| _____ | _____ |
| _____ | _____ |
| _____ | _____ |
| _____ | _____ |
| _____ | _____ |
| _____ | _____ |

# 3

## Friends who'll be there for you

*Stop swimming oceans for people who wouldn't*
*jump over a puddle for you*

In 2015, I won the fifteenth series of the UK television show *I'm a Celebrity . . . Get Me Out of Here!* Coming out of the jungle as a queen, and experiencing a totally different level of fame, was a wonderful but very difficult time for me. If you were 16–24 years old at the time you might have known who I was before the show, and 50/50 chances were you didn't like me or the idea of me. The rest of the nation probably didn't have a clue who I was. As far as most people were concerned, I was a complete reality television scumbag who was going to come bowling into their beloved television show slut-dropping, swearing and swigging Jägerbombs and ruin their precious jungle. And then they saw who I really was. They saw my caring side, my vulnerable side – they realised I don't take myself too seriously and I'm a real team player. And that is a feeling I'll never forget. Apparently, I received 80 per cent of the votes, which was just so mind-blowing when I think of all the big characters that were in there. Coming out of the jungle changed everything – suddenly a lot more people knew who I was and, like I say, most of them really embraced this new version of me. It was overwhelming to say the least. It was incredible, and super validating, and I thought it was all I had ever wanted – to essentially win a huge popularity contest. But the reality was that it was really daunting.

## Old friends are gold friends

During this time, I was super grateful for my old, real friends and family. When they got really pissed, a couple of them confessed, 'You know mate, I watched the whole lot and I had money on you winning.' They were really cute and so proud – but how they treated me, after I was named Queen of the Jungle, never changed. And how my mam treated me never changed. I remember coming home to Newcastle after Australia. My mam, my sister and a couple of my pals were all round my mam's house waiting to see me for the first time after I'd been on this two-week whirlwind promotional television tour, when I'd sat on the couch with Holly and Phil on *This Morning*, chatted with Piers Morgan, done every radio show you can think of, every photoshoot, all of it. I was in high demand and despite being overwhelmed I'd pushed myself to do absolutely everything that came my way. And then I got back to Newcastle and I'm expecting this hero's welcome, and I walk through the door and . . . nowt, nothing, not a dicky-bird, not so much as a poxy banner. I'm like 'Hello, I'm home!' and Laura is upstairs and says 'Hello, is that you?' and I say 'Yes, it's me!' and she replied, 'Okay, I'll be down in a second,' which was a bit lacklustre and not exactly what I was expecting but I rolled with it. Then my mam, who's also upstairs, shouts, 'Vicky? Is that you?' Again, I say 'Yes, it's me' – to which my mam replies, 'Good, the dishwasher needs emptying, can you empty it?'

I reply, 'Err, yeah, okay,' thinking what the hell?! No red carpet?! But actually, deep down, I felt so pleased in that moment, that my family and friends clearly weren't going to start treating me any differently, because I wouldn't have wanted them to. I was the same person I'd always been. And anyway, I can't stand sycophants. I know that I am who I am, which is normal and grounded, *because* no one close to me has ever said, 'You're the funniest, most talented person I know – I always knew you were going to win the jungle!' None of my close friends and family have ever licked my arse and that's why I am still bearable as a person. I'm really grateful to them. My friends, my real mates, my day ones, my ride-or-dies, my Laura, Natalie, Lyndsey, Steph, Kailee, those are the girls I've grown up with and no matter what – whether I'm winning the jungle or having to borrow twenty quid to go out because I've got nothing, they've always been there. And I'll never forget that. I'll never not be grateful to them.

Whenever I go back to see them in Newcastle, I can revert to how I have always been with them, and vice versa – and I think that being able to do that is a sign that they truly are good mates! It's like I never left. Even though after *I'm a Celebrity* I moved to London – where I'd been living in a totally different world where everyone is sucking me off, and I no longer have to wait in queues, and I'm going to fancy restaurants, openings, award shows, concerts and book signings – when I go home it feels like I've never been away. My old friends still treat me like I'm the Vicky who didn't have a pot to piss in when she finished university; the same Vicky who used to wear £1 dresses from Miss Selfridge because she was completely skint but didn't want to miss out on one drop of fun with the girlies. You can't put a price on those deep, authentic friendships, can you?

When I was away from my old mates, it was easy to lose sight of that person, the person I really was. I was overworked, overwhelmed, and again, unprepared. This time it was different to when I was on *Geordie Shore* – this time everyone liked me – but it was still hard. It was hard to keep my ego in check! I remember once, on a photoshoot, a makeup artist tried to put my shoes on for me. It sounds so stupid, but it sticks in my memory. I can still recall my thought process as they were trying to do it – that this was an incredibly surreal, daft situation, and that even though I was now more famous, more loved, I could still put my own bloody shoes on. All I'd done was survive a few weeks in a hot place feeling sticky and slightly uncomfortable with a few more kangaroo balls than I normally encountered. Still, it didn't sit well. I was going through a lot of inner turmoil and I needed people around me who were honest and kind. Down in London, in the industry I was in, they were proving hard to find. I didn't know how to spot them and it was starting to cause problems.

## All by myself

There were people at that time who only came into my life because of what I'd become, who wanted to ride the coat-tails of my new fame and what it was bringing me. I was so adamant that I wasn't going to let the fame go to my head and I was still going to be the same person that I had been before I went in the jungle that I regressed when I returned to the UK. I held myself back in loads of ways, out of fear more than anything. I refused to elevate at all. To a certain extent, when you come out of something like *I'm a Celebrity* you should up your game, you should step up to the fame and grow. There are more eyes on you so you need to fix yourself up. Even if you were a bit of a party person before you must embrace a more family-friendly image and do better. But I was so determined to keep my feet on the ground, I regressed, and started going out more, and knocked around with people who were, honestly, probably better suited to the image I had when I was in *Geordie Shore*, and not suited at all to this new side of me I wanted people to see: the caring, kind and intelligent Vicky.

It took me a while to work out who they were. My move to London was a huge transition for me. I was trying to cope with the move and the fact I was so far away from my friends and family, the very people who'd helped to keep me normal, grounded and happy. I was also dealing with the intense attention from the press. On top of that, there were lots of people coming into my life who, in retrospect, I can see were there for all the wrong reasons. It was a lot of change and, looking back, I didn't make the best decisions.

I understand now my naivety was probably because

I was lonely. Amazing things were happening to me but I didn't have people to share it with. Apart from a couple of good mates, Gav and Alex, I didn't really have anyone I could trust down there in London, so I ended up knocking about with people who weren't really right for me and going out with boys that weren't really right. There's that saying, 'loneliness isn't really about being on your own, it's the feeling that nobody cares', and everyone expected me to be riding high, buzzing like an old fridge off my success and the new-found fame that had come my way, but actually I just felt so scared, and so lonely. I remember being in a room full of people and realising that no one in it really cared about me. They just saw me as something that was hot, the current flavour of the month. I mean, I'm not stupid – I may have been incredibly naïve – but I still knew what was going on and I knew it wasn't right. You can feel who really cares about you, and who really doesn't, when you give yourself a chance to. Being surrounded by people and knowing they don't care, that's my definition of loneliness. I experienced some of the most heartbreaking loneliness of my life straight after winning the jungle, while putting on this façade that I was having the best time of my life – and I know I did such a good job of it that everyone had no idea I was in pain. They just assumed I was super, super happy.

And of course, I ended up getting hurt. There are

some things in life you just can't be told, you can't be warned off and you can't spot a mile off. Sometimes in life you have to learn from your mistakes and that is the only way you are going to learn. I think learning who is a true friend and who you can trust is one of those things. Now, I can see these people heading in my direction and think, *you're going to be trouble*, but back then, I just took everyone at face value. I've always been candid, to my detriment. Everyone knows exactly where they stand with me and I'm honest to a fault – I mean, please don't ever tell me a secret because I cannot keep it. I tell all my friends 'Don't tell me anything', so I'm always the last to know their news. This is a punch in the dick as I love good news but honestly, it's all I deserve for being so loose lipped. I just assumed everyone was honest and trustworthy like me, and finding out that people weren't is a very hard lesson to learn.

## Fair-weather friends

I had a couple of bad experiences with new female friends during this time, in moments when I was trying to keep a low profile. I would want to go out somewhere quiet, with a few girl mates, and not have to worry about being seen or papped. Then, just before we'd arrive one of them would say, 'Oh, I don't know how it happened, but the paparazzi have found out we're here,' and I'd think, *no, you know exactly how, don't you, hon?* Or worse still, I'd find that parts of my life that no one except a few close friends knew about would pop up in the press.

There was this one particular story that made me realise what was going on. At the time, the press was obsessed with my love life because – heaven forbid! – I could be a strong, successful woman who didn't need a man. I couldn't be riding high off the back of my jungle win – busy and happy being single. No, no, no – I must be after a fella. The papers were consumed with it, so every man I was seen with I was romantically linked to. And I remember saying to a small handful of people, maybe three max, that I felt like I couldn't trust any men any more, because they all seemed to be using me to get somewhere. I started moaning that I didn't know if anyone would ever love me for me, and questioning out loud if I was always going to have to second-guess myself and any man who came near me. Would I ever be able to just walk into a bar again and think that lad fancies me for me? I didn't know. I admitted to them I was terrified of being on my own forever, but I couldn't leave and go back up north for some normality because I was so overworked, and I knew if I stopped and went home to recuperate, my worried mam wouldn't let me come back again. I needed to be successful. I needed to be in London. So, I stayed and things got worse.

I thought sharing my fears with some of my new friends, confiding in people I thought I could trust, would help. But you guessed it, the story miraculously turned up in the press. And it was so painful because they were my innermost thoughts – my thoughts about not being able to trust people and worrying about being alone and unlovable – exposed for the world to see. How those *friends* proved me right! In retrospect I see it was almost poetic in its irony but back then I just felt hurt and stupid. I felt more alone than ever before and like there was absolutely no one in the city I could trust. It was a painful way to learn that lesson, but I had to learn it on my own. It didn't matter that my mam had been saying to me for ages, 'Why are you hanging around with those people?' or that my sister had been saying, 'I've never met them but I can tell they're a bunch of knobs!' Even my agents were like, 'Vicky, you've finally got a great reputation and you're surrounding yourself with awful people – you're undoing all of our hard work.' Yes, all these amazing women had given me great advice, but this is just one of life's lessons that I had to learn for myself.

Maybe I was using those people as much as they were using me, as an excuse not to be brave and up my game, as a security blanket, and they were using me to jump queues and get freebies. Maybe we were both as bad as each other.

It took me being burned to let go of that childish, defensive behaviour. There was a slow build-up to working out which people were taking advantage of me and who really had good intentions. During this lonely confusion, I saw old habits raise their ugly heads, the same bad habits I had in *Geordie Shore* when I would drink to self-medicate. I started to rely heavily on alcohol. It was unhealthy, and inexplicable – I'd finally got everything I've ever wanted and here I was, self-sabotaging. It took a series of really close calls, silly mistakes and upsetting situations where I was let down and I let myself down to make me realise I was on the cusp of fucking this all up again for myself. I knew why I was doing it: I felt I wasn't good enough, I felt I didn't deserve what I had, and that at any moment I was going to wake up from this jungle dream and everyone would remember that I was that girl who had *that* fight in *that* nightclub, and I was *that* person who swore all the time, and I was *that* person who had sex on television. I was terrified. I hid all those emotions from myself and the world with drink, and thought if I surrounded myself with the sort of people who don't want you to be better, who don't really care about you or ask too many questions, that my relapse could go unnoticed and it would make me feel better. But it didn't. And I knew I needed to get better friends in my new life.

## The Igniters, the Draggers and the Middle-of-the-Roads

Just before I went into the jungle, I started seeing two therapists. Nick and Eva Speakman were renowned for their work on fighting phobias, which is how my agents convinced me into going to see them. They said, 'You're going into the jungle, you're going to need to prepare yourself for all the bugs, creepy-crawlies and downright disgusting critters.' I thought they were being silly; I was so excited to be given this opportunity I couldn't see a downside and, besides, I didn't think I was scared of anything. But it wasn't the bugs my agents were worried about. I laugh now about the person I was when the Speakmans first met me. We've ended up being good friends and I love them so much for all that they've taught me and all the times they've been there for me, so our relationship has become a really easy one that brings me so much joy. 'You were so angry,' they remind me, and I was! I was angry that my agents thought I needed help, and I was angry because I was exhausted and in the middle of a book tour and I had to be there when I could have been in bed getting a bit of a lie in. I was so defensive and agitated. But, after my first hour with them, all my defences crumbled and true work could begin. My agents hadn't booked that session because they wanted me to conquer my fear of cockroaches, they'd booked it because they knew I was about to be put in another situation where I was out of control, and they didn't want me to feel how I'd felt when I was in *Geordie Shore*. My agents Gemma and Nadia at Mokkingbird helped me when I couldn't even help myself – and I've remained with them ever since. Their kindness is why I've stuck around and today they are so much more than just my agents. They are my friends, and I am so grateful to them for believing in me when no one else did – but also for making me get the help I needed, however sneaky their methods were! Alongside the Mokkingbird girlies, the Speakmans have remained a constant in my life, and every time I've felt low, anytime I'm seeing old self-sabotaging habits creep back in, or there are any signs I'm becoming who I don't want to be again, they help me get back on track. They were the ones who taught me about the different kinds of friends everyone has in their life.

They divided friends into three groups: the Igniters, the Draggers and the Middle-of-the-Roads. And they told me that you know if you have a good friend in your life by how you feel in your heart when they call you and you see their name pop up on your screen. It's so simple but it's so true.

For example, I had pals, then, in those early days down in London, who would ring me and I just knew they'd be after something, 'I need somewhere to stay in London,' they'd say, or 'I need tickets for this', 'I can't get into this nightclub' or 'Do you know this person?' They'd never call because they were genuinely interested in what I was up to, or calling to help me, or just to check in and make sure I was happy. And I'd know it the minute their name flashed up on my phone and my whole body would tense up and I wouldn't want to answer. They are the Draggers.

Then you have others who when they call you, you feel good. They don't understand what you're going through, but you don't need them to. You get where they fit into your life – they're kind, they mean well and their hearts are in the right place. They make you feel okay, they don't rock your boat, and they don't give or take to your overall mood. They are the Middle-of-the-Roads.

But then you have those people – those magical, shiny people – who when you see their name flash up on your mobile, your whole body buzzes and you literally light up from the inside out like your phone screen. One conversation with them can make you feel like you're capable of anything. For example, if you tell them you're going to try to eat healthier, they say, 'Fucking hell, yes, I'm going to give that a go as well – let's be healthy together! We'll smash it so when we're on our holidays we can eat whatever we want!' Or if you're sad and feeling low and need a treat and a chat, they say, 'Right, I'm coming over, we're going to open a bottle of wine and put the world to rights!' The fact that we as human beings have the ability to be someone's sunshine, to make them happy, to pick them up when they are feeling low – I think it's incredible and we should all respect that power and we should all aspire to be Igniters. I know I do.

This phone test my therapists taught me really reminds me how to recognise on a daily basis who is good for me and who isn't. It's crazy but when I see my boyfriend's name pop up on my phone, I come over all gooey and giddy, even if we had a row in the morning because he's left his dirty pants everywhere. When I see my sister's name, I will drop anything to pick up that phone because I know she needs me – just as I need her. Sometimes she's good for my mental health, she's good for my soul. All Igniters are! And we all need more Igniters in our lives – people that spark joy into your heart and make you feel love and happiness in every single one of your extremities. The Sarahs, the Gavs, the Hannahs of this world. They make you feel alive and remind you why you have friends in the first place.

But the Draggers . . . they are people who you know take from you and will deplete you of energy. Now I've described them to you, do you know who they are in your life? You can convince yourself for so long that they are proper friends, and I did too! But these friendships are one-sided, based on one person taking everything they can from you and draining you of love and energy and giving you nothing in return. The problem is, I was one of those people who liked a wounded bird type, who thought she could help everyone. I used to tell myself, *I can fix them, make them be more stable, more adjusted, get them on this ladder, help them with this job.* But I couldn't, and sadly, neither can you. They just take from you and take from you, and drag you down to their level. As you get older, I think it gets easier to recognise these types and you include less and less of them in your life. You become savvier. You get too tired to put up with other people's bullshit. You know your worth as well. Even if you still struggle with low self-esteem, I'm hopeful you recognise your true value more and more as you tick off each birthday, more than maybe you did when you were a kid or a teenager, and you don't let a lot of those people in your life anymore. Because you deserve more, you deserve friendships based on trust, love and mutual respect – not just what one can do for another. Not today, Satan, not today!

## Ending toxic friendships

The big problem is when these so-called friends have been in your life for a long time. I think over the last couple of years, when I've started to get a bit of a handle on the bigger things in my own life, things that I can change and control, I've then been able pay attention to the people I have around me and get to grips with the fact I've still got some people in my life who shouldn't be in it – 'friends' who I know are not the best for me, but who I've kept in my life because I've known them forever, and they knew me when I had nothing. I have an unwavering, almost naïve loyalty to people who wouldn't show it to me, who I know are only still around because I can give them something.

I'm just not cutthroat. I'm never going to be one of those people who can say 'You don't bring me peace, so fuck off out of my life!' I take my hat off to people that can be that savage because I imagine their lives are quite straightforward, but I'm not that cold. I'm a total fanny and I'm as loyal as a dog, which is why I've stayed in relationships that were wrong for me for too long, stayed in jobs that weren't right and was hurt by people who were meant to care about me. When I know I have to clear out some of these people who have been in my life a while but I know deep down are not good for me I just try to distance myself a little bit. You don't have to be Alan Sugar on *The Apprentice*, firing your friends left, right and centre – we can't all be that direct and hurtful – but you can easily remove yourself.

How? If you have some people you need to distance yourself from, just don't reach out to them – through habit or obligation. Trim down your communication. And if they reach out to you, asking to make plans, don't commit to anything. Tell them how busy or stressed you are at the moment; tell them you're focusing on yourself – tell them the truth, that you're focusing on you and your needs. Having a bit of personal self-care. And you know what? They'll get the hint. They've proven they're not great friends time and time again, so they won't keep pursuing you that hard – and the peace you find when you are finally free from those people who were not supporting you, or who were making you feel bad about yourself, or who are trying to bring you down to their level ... there's no feeling like it. Protecting my peace of mind is all that I'm about in my thirties, and I would love you to try it, too.

## How to be a fabulous friend

I've always considered myself to be a good friend because I'm fiercely loyal. I don't know whether it's because I'm a Scorpio (I can literally sense half of you rolling your eyes as you read that sentence. I am so sorry, but I do believe in star signs, I'm afraid). I have certain characteristics attached to that horoscope, good and bad ones – if you cross me, I'll never forget it, but if you're a friend, I'll go into battle for you. I've always considered myself to be a good mate but what I consider that to be has changed over recent years. I used to think it was being really honest, saying things like 'I wouldn't fucking wear that, mate,' justifying my comments by telling whoever they were directed to, 'I just tell it how it is!' But, actually, now that I'm older I understand being a good friend is about being kind and gentle. Yes, being honest, but being tactful with it and being that person in their life who says the positive things that you wish they would say to themselves.

Some of my mates are amazing but I know they don't see what I see. When I look at them, I see beautiful brave women doing things their own way, or incredibly strong people choosing their own path, or I see someone who is dealing with so much pain behind the scenes but is keeping a brave face on it, or I see someone trying something new and getting judged for it but keeping at it. All my friends are doing these amazing things for themselves and now I tell them how proud I am of them every chance I get. I used to be afraid to share my feelings, to really tell my friends how much I loved them, but now I can't tell them enough, or show them enough how much I care. It is never enough. Always share what is in your heart to make a friend feel better.

## The lessons found in loss

I lost my best friend in June 2018, when he was just thirty-seven. Paul was the glue that stuck my Newcastle friendship group together. He always had so much time for everyone else, and he had this larger-than-life personality, but it wasn't until after he'd gone that we truly realised how much we loved him. The day we found out he'd died, we sat together, in deep shock, showing each other our last messages from him. He always used to message out of the blue, checking in on us. He was doing that whole 'make sure your friends are okay' check-in before it ever became a thing on social media. He was just thoughtful. I know we tend to rose-tint and romanticise loved ones when they're gone, but I'm not doing that. He was a sassy bastard and you wouldn't want to cross him, but he was also the best friend you could ever ask for. And losing someone like that makes you realise what's important – it's not having a million different friends to go out with, or loads of people on your phone, or famous mates … it's having people that fucking ask if you're okay and genuinely care about the answer!

Paul's death was a huge wake-up call for our entire friendship group, and since losing him I've endeavoured to be the best friend I can be. I know in life we all have to come to terms with loss and living with grief, but I don't want to lose someone else so young again, and it's made me so appreciative of every moment with my friends. That deep pain we experienced was a pivotal moment for me and all of my mates. It's bittersweet, but heartbreak and hard times do bring people closer together, and since then I've tried to be more like Paul. I'm away from Newcastle so much, but when I'm back, my friends know I'm back! I always plan a party, and I always throw whoever is having a baby a baby shower – and, honestly, when you're in your thirties there's always a fucking baby shower. I organise the whip-rounds for the girls for their birthdays, and if someone is quiet in the group chat, I quietly message them to make sure they're okay. I have realised in the last few years through the experiences of being lonely, then having bad friends, and then losing a real friend, just how priceless amazing people who have your back are – and how we all need to direct our energy towards who is important.

The most upsetting thing about losing Paul is he'd be so proud of the group of friends we are now. We weren't drifting apart, but we were getting consumed with our own lives, which I know is natural – coupling up, moving away with partners, having babies. We'd see each other at Christmas and get together for a couple of birthdays every year, but it wasn't that regular. Now, we see each other once a month.

We make sure of it. It's so sad it had to take losing Paul, but it made us realise how important we all are to one another, and now there's not a birthday that goes by without a celebration, or a milestone that goes by without recognition. People get flowers for everything – my local florist literally knows me by name – and we're closer than ever. He'd be so proud of us. *I'm* proud of us.

We've helped each other work through our grief in very different ways. When it first happened, there were a couple of girls who shut themselves off from the rest of us. They didn't know how to process what was happening, they didn't want to believe it and I understood those emotions and felt similarly. I talked to my therapists about my grief, about how I should be grieving, and they asked me a really poignant question: what was Paul like? I told them he was the biggest attention seeker going; that he was Mr Newcastle, a massive gay fella who I met while I was hosting at all the local nightclubs. I told them he knew everyone's gossip, and everyone loved him, that he was always there and up for a night out. I told them that losing him made it impossible for me to go home; that I was skipping time in Newcastle because without him it didn't feel like Newcastle anymore. All I could focus on when I had nights out with my friends, among these same, lovely faces, was the empty seat, and the person that was missing. And I couldn't cope.

'Vicky, we understand your pain, but you're making Paul's death about you, when it isn't. It's about Paul. What would he want you to do?' asked one of my therapists.

Paul would want to be remembered and toasted on every single night out. He'd want us to sit and laugh about the silly situations we'd got ourselves into – the terrible eyebrow waxes, the nightclub scrapes, legendary after-parties and the horrific hangovers! And he would want to be remembered how he was: this hilarious, kind, warm and vibrant man. That was the best advice I ever got, because once I got up to Newcastle, I threw myself into my friendships, and we talk about him all the time. Yes, we cry, but he'd probably like that as well – to know he was loved and to know he is missed. We check in on his mam, see if Jackie's okay. I send her flowers on Mother's Day. I don't hide from his memory. I embrace it and do him justice.

That's what helped us – leaning on each other, and remembering him. He was such a huge part of my life and I won't do him justice by forgetting about him. I celebrate him. The pain doesn't go away. For his last birthday I organised a Zoom call to toast him, but on the day I lost my head and proper went to ground. I could see all the lasses chatting in the group, but I really missed him and couldn't see past my pain! But sometimes you need to feel your feels. Some days I miss him so much and I feel guilty that everyone's having kids and falling in love and getting promoted and he didn't get to do that. On his birthday, I had a day to myself, and explained myself to the girls the next day.

'I feel I let yous down,' I apologised. 'I wanted to be there for you so much and to remember Paul but I just felt sad, because we're all moving on and he's not.' Again, they all came to my rescue, messaging me saying never worry about feeling like this, thanking me for doing so much for them, reminding me how much they loved me. Paul wouldn't want us to feel terrible. We know that. He had a fun life. It wasn't long enough, but we've had to try to accept that sometimes things aren't fair. That he was just too good for this world. When you go through a traumatic event with a group of friends, you're bonded in a different way for the rest of your life. Although losing someone is horrific, and I wish things were different, you can't ignore the things that come out of it – the painful and the beautiful – and one of the things my group took out of it is that we're so appreciative of our friendship now.

## Hitting the jackpot

Even though I don't see them every day, I know my girls have got my back. I also know the only time in my life I sound smug is when I talk about my mates, because I feel like I've hit the jackpot. They are strong, opinionated, sassy women who aren't afraid to do things their way, and who are as beautiful on the inside as they are on the outside. They would go into battle for me. When times were hard and people didn't like me, they would stand up for me. I suppose that's how I know they're good mates. Because even your own shadow leaves you in the darkness, but a real mate never leaves your side.

I remember back in the day, when I had nothing – I was completely skint, on the bones of my arse – and one friend took out a Provident loan, or a 'provvy loan' as we called them back then. She was as skint as I was, but she knew I'd just broken up with my boyfriend and I needed cheering up. And those loans were terrible as well, you had to pay back so much interest it was disgraceful, but she did it for me. That was twelve years ago but I still remember that moment, and that friend being there for me. Obviously, I'm older and wiser now and I definitely would not recommend *that* particular financial decision, but the gesture was so kind. Now I'm in a position where I do have a little bit more, I make sure my friends don't want for anything. If there's ever someone who needs help with a house deposit, or a birthday party, or to borrow clothes, or get a nice reservation at a restaurant, I make sure I'm there for them because they were there for me when

I needed them. We're all so lucky to have each other and we know it.

There's that expression: you are a complete reflection of the five people you spend the most time with. Who are your five and what do they say about you? We should all look around at who those people are for us, and what they bring to our lives, who they help us become. The other day, me and my mam had a chat on the phone about it:

'I want you to be one of mine!' she told me.

'You don't get to pick them, mam, it's who you spend the most time with.'

'No,' she responded, 'you'll be one of mine, because you're dead thoughtful, you're really positive and you're excited for life, so I want you to be one of mine.'

I just don't think compliments get better than that, do they? My mam is definitely one of mine, she reminds me to be humble and grateful, but also to own my power. So many people just want you to be small and timid; overly grateful for everything and self-deprecating to a fault. Some people want you to shrink. But not my mam, she encourages me to stand tall and reminds me every so often that yes, I did this. Yes, I've had good luck, and brilliant agents and played a blinder in the jungle but ultimately, I didn't give up or stop, I refused to let the doubters faze me and the darkness consume me and I kept going. And she always reminds me of that.

You have to look at your friends, at who you spend the most time with, and know they are going to shape you. You're crackers if you think you can be around a happy, smiley, positive and kind person day in, day out and they're not going to rub off on you. It's just not possible. Sadly, this works the other way too. I used to have someone in my life and I hadn't realised how much of an effect their presence had on me. We had a prolonged period of absence from each other, and I found I was less anxious, less stressed and more positive as a result. It's so important to try and recognise those people in your life that have a negative impact and make positive changes. Sometimes it is not always possible to remove them completely, but at least when you see them you can have your guard up and be prepared for the negativity and then brush it off as a result.

At the other end of the spectrum, notice how you feel when you surround yourself with positive, kind people. You become more positive, you become kinder. It's easy to become complacent after being in this industry for ten years, but when someone comes along who it's still new and exciting for, who says, 'Bloody hell, I just met so and so,' or 'Can you believe they just asked for your picture?' it reminds me that my life is exciting, that people can be great and that I'm lucky. Be with people who make you excited, who make you grateful, who make you happy. And when your friends aren't feeling happy themselves, be there for them, to listen and support them. It's that simple.

## Be a friend to yourself

In any walk of life, not just in the public eye, there are people who want the best for you – and those who don't. Those who nurture you – and those who view you as the competition, or want to hold you down. We've all known people, friends, colleagues who will step on you to get where they need to go, and part of growing up is working out who is good for you, who isn't, and distancing yourself from the people who don't have your best interests at heart. When I first got into the industry, I loved nothing more than being papped with a famous friend on my arm, being captured on a fancy night out with other celebrities. I got a real kick out of seeing myself on Mail Online the next day (cringe!) but now I don't have any of those tabloid apps on my phone. I deleted them for a number of reasons. First, it's not great to see photos of yourself all the time that you didn't know were being taken and have no control over. You're never going to like them and you're always going to end up feeling bad about yourself. Second, I deleted them because the stories were hardly ever true. It's confus-ing to read all these untruths about yourself and get a conflicted image of who you really are. I was also sick of reading stuff about my mates. I know loads of lovely people in the industry, who I seriously rate, and it was hard for me to read stories about them that I knew weren't true – or worse, stuff that I knew was true and painful, and they were trying to deal with privately, that didn't need to be splashed about for entertainment.

How I feel about fame and famous friends has definitely changed loads over the years. I want different things out of my job now. I've always wanted to be successful, I've always wanted to be rich – and I'm really not sorry to say either of those things, even though I know it's tacky to admit the money thing. But I want to change the discourse around that. If a man says he wants to be rich, or even famous, he'll be patted on the back and congratulated for being a straight shooter; he'll be declared one to watch – ambitious, driven, the next big thing. But when a woman admits it, like I just have, for some reason all these negative connotations pop up. We need to flip that script. I don't want to be rich for vapid reasons. I don't desire a wardrobe full of designer gear or fancy watches on my wrist or fast cars on my driveway; I want to live in a nice house and to look after my mam and my sister. I'm not sorry about my goals, and I sure as hell won't apologise for being driven or determined, but they have changed in the last five years. Now I realise that if I could have got to where I am today any other way, as quickly as I have, I would have loved to. Because deep down, I'm not sure I'm cut out for this type of fame. I'm very sensitive, and I'm quite boring. And I don't think either of those make you a very good famous person. Subsequently, I'm a celebrity that doesn't have many celebrity friends. I keep my group small and safe, and I treasure the friends that slip into it.

I'd advise you to be choosy with your mates. They reflect you. And if you've been hanging around with a bunch of self-centred twats, people will assume you're a self-centred twat too – even if you're not! Now don't get me wrong, I don't want anyone reading this to go on a crazy cull, getting rid of anyone who's ever made them feel bad – we all have crap days, and we all deserve a second chance. Sometimes we can go through a couple of years when we're not happy with ourselves, and find it hard to be a good friend to anyone else. But that's where loyalty comes into play, and where you need to work out if it is just a stage for them, and if you can help, or if they deserve you. Don't be too harsh or cutthroat, but do trust your gut and listen for the warning bells. If a friend fucks up once, fair play, but if it happens again and again, you need to protect yourself. Once is a mistake, twice is a pattern and three times is a habit. And there is no place in your life for people with bad friendship habits.

Often with people who claim to be your friend, you can't listen to what they say, you have to watch what they do. If someone tells you over and over again that they love you but they are hurting you, or making you feel bad about yourself, or making you question yourself, then they don't love you – it's that simple. If someone is saying to you, 'I am one of your best mates' – and believe me I've had this happen to me a few times – and 'There's nothing I wouldn't do for you,' but never put their hand in their pocket to pay for anything, if they expect the world from you but are never there when you need them and don't listen to your problems, pay attention. It's their behaviour you need to take notice of. So, if you're ever questioning if someone is a real friend, or if they deserve you going that extra mile for them, true love is about actions not words. They answer your call, don't let it go to voicemail; they send you encouraging texts on important occasions; and they do little things to cheer you up when they know you've had a rough time of it, be it meeting you for a coffee, sending you a card, or planning something to look forward to.

## Wonder women

I have a brilliant mam, a strong sister and amazing friends – I'm surrounded by superwomen and I feel very lucky. Most women can relate to the idea that behind every strong woman is a tribe of even stronger women who you know have your back, and can help you survive. We should own that, honour that, celebrate it. I don't hate men and I have many beautiful male influences in my life, but we get something from other women that is irreplaceable. It's important to nurture those relationships, even when we become mothers and wives, or CEOs, or celebrities – never forget that you are a daughter, a sister and a friend first. I know some people who get so caught up in being a mother they almost lose their identities, or are so busy climbing the corporate ladder they forget to pull their friends up with them.

I urge you to remember who has been there for you in the past, before everything and everyone else, when you were single and crying in the nightclub toilets that you were never going to find anyone, or eating a grab bag of Maltesers on the sofa after a rough day at the office . . . it was your girls. Reward loyalty, and match it. There's nothing I wouldn't do for those women, and it's returned tenfold. My loving energy is matched, and so will yours be. Give as much attention to your friends as you would a romantic relationship. There is true love in real friendships.

# The Secret To... filling your life with people you love

Make sure you engage with people who pull the magic out of you ... and disengage from those who squash it. Filling your diary with people you love, who you know love you in return, will not only protect your peace, but boost your mood 24/7. Indeed, cherish friends who:

* Listen to understand you, not just listen for their turn to speak. Too often we don't have real conversations with friends, we just embark on a battle for airtime, not properly taking on board what the other person has shared. Think about what they've actually said, and respond with empathy;

* Check in with you – and not because they need something but because they genuinely care about you. The friend who just reaches out when they need a babysitter, or an in with your new boss, or someone to go drinking with, is not a real friend at all;

* Value your time, energy and opinions. They keep their promises and don't let you down, or

keep you waiting without explanation, and give you space to share, free of judgement – offering advice and solutions, or just a sounding board. A good friend allows you to be you, and values what you are – there are no needs for airs and graces, or putting on a show. You accept each other;

* Celebrate your wins, commiserate your losses and are not competitive with you – nothing drains a happy friendship like envy or jealousy. A true friend will be happy for your good luck and enjoy your good times, as you are for theirs, and would never gloat or say 'I told you so' when things don't go your way;

* . . . and allow you to do all of the above for them! Friends who let you share in their good times boost your own happiness, because giving attention and affection is a real serotonin boost. It feels good to be a good friend, that's a fact.

* Oh, and cherish friends who bring you wine and snacks (this one is very important) but protect your peace – don't let toxic people drag you down. It's hard, but you must close some doors if they take you down bad friendship paths.

## PREPARE YOUR PURPOSE

Grab a pencil and make a list of all the people who are currently in your life – it can be the five you see most, like I discussed in this chapter, or your wider circle. Below, split them into three lists: your Draggers, your Middle-of-the-Roads and your Igniters. As you write out each name, think about the memories you've shared and how they make you feel. If they've excited, enthralled and/or understood you, bathe in gratitude and make a note to tell them soon how much they mean to you – even a text will do! If, when you look at their name, your reaction isn't so positive, and you feel pain, cross through it, wishing them well, but making a promise to yourself to see them less, to protect yourself from them and erase their negativity from your life.

The people in my life are . . .

| Draggers | Middle-of-the-Roads | Igniters |
|----------|---------------------|----------|
| _____ | _____ | _____ |
| _____ | _____ | _____ |
| _____ | _____ | _____ |

| Draggers | Middle-of-the-Roads | Igniters |
|---|---|---|
| _____ | _____ | _____ |
| _____ | _____ | _____ |
| _____ | _____ | _____ |
| _____ | _____ | _____ |
| _____ | _____ | _____ |
| _____ | _____ | _____ |
| _____ | _____ | _____ |
| _____ | _____ | _____ |
| _____ | _____ | _____ |
| _____ | _____ | _____ |
| _____ | _____ | _____ |
| _____ | _____ | _____ |

# 4

## Family . . . the friends you can't pick

*Family is anyone that loves you unconditionally.*

Family is very important to me, but family life hasn't always been easy. I'm sure you'll understand what I mean when I say that I find relationships with my relatives both beautiful and sometimes incredibly difficult to navigate. Today, I have a brilliant relationship with my mam, my sister and my dad, but it hasn't always been that way. And that's the thing we all need to remember about families: the dynamics change and evolve, and the people within them grow, or change and evolve, at different times over the years. Families are not static, however much we may wish them to be. They can't always look the same way they did when we were little. I think one of the biggest things about families I had to work out as I got older is that even though your family members may be secondary characters in your play – your parents, your siblings, your cousins (and they may all play their supporting roles really well), they're the protagonists in their own story, too. We don't necessarily acknowledge this when we're younger. Your parents and siblings are their own people with their own aims, likes, dislikes and boundaries. With their own problems. They do not exist to orbit around you, precious little star. It's a tough lesson to learn, that one, if you have a bit of narcissist in you ... which I definitely do.

## A mother's love

A mother–daughter relationship is precious for most women. It doesn't need to be a biological mother, it can be a mother figure or role model you have in your life, an auntie, a grandmother, a good friend – a boss even. My relationship with my mam has been incredibly complicated over the years. People see us now and think it's always been how it is today and we're truly blessed and very lucky – which is true to a certain extent, I am grateful every day for my mam. But it hasn't always been this way. I've gone through all the same things that everyone goes through with their mam, and then some. The power struggle began when I was a teenager, like most mother-and-daughter power struggles do, and it wasn't anything out of the ordinary – it was all your usual, run-of-the-mill mother-and-daughter disagreements. I wanted to go out in miniskirts and boob tubes in the height of winter and my mam wanted me in a parka jacket and ski pants. I wanted my first boyfriend to be allowed to stay the night but my mam would have preferred me locked up in a nunnery until I was sixty-seven. She wanted me to keep my room tidy and help a little bit around the house and I wanted to live a carefree and rent-free existence in her home while she ran around after me and attended to my every whim while feeding me peeled grapes. You know, the usual stuff. Cue all the classic Kevin and Perry-style strops – 'just let me live my life', 'I am not your slave', 'this is so unfair', blah blah blah. I was full of adolescent insolence and angst, not to mention I had a real flair for the dramatics, so absolutely everything was the end of the world.

Looking back, I think I first started to appreciate my mam when I was at university. She bailed me out of loads of financially difficult situations without rubbing my nose in my silly mistakes. Whenever I'd go home, it was always just so lovely to catch up with her and get looked after for a bit. I remember that's when I realised how much she did for me. When you have to stand on your own two feet for the first time and you see how difficult it is, you fully appreciate the gravity of everything your mam has been doing for you for so long. I have vivid memories of going back to Liverpool after a weekend at home, and getting whacked on the National Express for eight hours as it was all I could afford, and I'd sit on the coach sobbing. I loved uni, but leaving my mam, and leaving home, it broke my heart every time we had to say goodbye.

Just when we'd gotten over those awful, awkward teenage years and it seemed as though my time at uni had matured me and repaired our relationship, along came *Geordie Shore*. The show almost ruined our relationship forever and virtually left us estranged by the end. This was a really difficult time for us, and if I hadn't left the show when I did, I don't know if our relationship would have ever recovered. She used to work at the local paper, and when the show first came out, the *Chronicle* had to reflect the voices of lots of the locals who hated us for glamorising binge drinking and bed hopping, for our aggressive behaviour, and for stereotyping a whole region. My mam would hide from people at work when I'd done something stupid on the show, and unless people actually knew we were related she wouldn't admit it. Not only did I make our personal relationship hard for ages, but I made her professional life hard for a long time, too. As a kid you just think your mam should always take your side – 'who cares what they think, you're my mam!' But now, as an adult, I can see I put her in a terribly awkward position and was being quite selfish. I wasn't in a nice position myself but I never once stopped to think about how my behaviour was affecting her career, as I was in deep pursuit of mine. My mam really struggled with the way I behaved on *Geordie Shore* and with what the show was doing to me. Each time I went away to film a series, I'd come back and she'd recognise less and less of her once intelligent and kind daughter. I knew I was letting her down but I was just so caught up in it all, I didn't see a way out.

But of course there was, and luckily for me, I got the second chance I needed – not only with the British public but with my mam too, in the form of *I'm a Celebrity . . . Get Me Out of Here!*. When I came out of the jungle years later, it was so lovely for my mam to have the country see the daughter she always knew I was. I'm not a mother (unless you count Milo, my Labrador, which by the way I 100 per cent do!) so I can't really imagine how awful it must have been to have people tell you that your daughter is a scumbag and a monster, and then how wonderful it must be to have everyone change their opinion. I think she got a great sense of vindication, almost like 'See! I fucking told you she was nice!' That's probably been one of the greatest decisions of my life – leaving *Geordie Shore*. Not only for my career and for my mental health, but also because it allowed me to go on to win the jungle and repair my relationship with my mother.

## More than just a mam

As adult children, we need to stop thinking of our mums as being one-dimensional, as if their only role is to be our mother. They are women with a million roles to play. I used to introduce her to people rather dismissively, saying, 'This is my mam,' and she'd say 'Actually, I'm Caroll!' I realise now I was reducing her to one role, making *her* all about *me*. For many women motherhood is all they want, but for most women it's just a small part of who they are. I didn't realise until very recently that even though I said it with pride − 'this is the woman who made me, she's the best' − I was actually stripping my mam of a huge part of her identity. It's only when you get older, or you have kids yourself, or you just become a bit more evolved, you can see your mother as more than a supporting character in your life. She's the leading lady in her own life, and you're actually a secondary character in hers. We're all so self-absorbed when we're young that it's difficult to see the woman who raised you as anything other than your mam. We need to try, though, and give them the recognition they deserve.

Our relationship has got loads better since I gave her the credit she deserves as a human. She is such a strong woman. When I was going through the nightclub fight back in 2013 − before the jungle − and the subsequent court case, I was mad at her for not giving me all her support. I used to shout about her abandoning me. I'd say it to my sister, and to my friends, and I felt so much resentment, such bitterness. Eventually, my sister said, 'Why don't you tell her?' The truth is I was a bit of fanny and was terrified of confrontation with my mam. But eventually I got up the courage to tell her how hurtful it was. 'I've always loved you, but I hated that you abandoned me then,' I said.

'I'm so sorry I left you,' she told me, 'but I was dealing with so much at the time.'

What I hadn't truly comprehended was that as I was being arrested at her house and the police were searching her entire home while she was there, she was also going through so much in her personal life. My dad isn't well; he has had issues with alcohol his whole life and sometimes he has more control over his addiction than others. But at that particular time, he had completely lost control and it was very difficult for us as a family to just watch him try and drink himself to death. My mam was dealing with this and facing the very sobering prospect that her marriage was over. She'd done such a good job of hiding how bad things were from us, and all her friends and family, for so many years, taking all that pain and shame on her own shoulders, and she literally couldn't do it anymore – and on top of all this she was expected to deal with my drama as well.

'I was trying to save my marriage,' she explained to me that day, 'and I was trying to look after your dad who was so unwell, and I just couldn't save you. I was losing you and there was nothing I could do about any of it. I regret it and I'm sorry.'

And there I was, mad because I wasn't the centre of her universe. Dickhead. Looking back, I feel terribly ashamed of myself – not only because of what I put her through, but because of how little support I offered her at the time. I accepted her apology, and I've apologised profusely to her over the years for not being the girl she brought up. As I say, the minute you start to see your mother as more than just a character in your own play, that's when you can begin to heal rifts, mend relationships and support each other. But it takes work.

## Show yourself

I think transparency between mothers and their children is really crucial, but I know lots of people who are scared for their mam to know who they really are. I've had friends get papped with me and suddenly a cigarette is chucked across the street.

'What are you doing?' I'd ask.

'My mam doesn't know I smoke.'

'What!' I respond, shocked, 'you're in your fucking thirties, mate. What the hell? I'd understand if you were fifteen and behind a bike shed, but you're thirty-two!'

There is nothing my mum doesn't know about me – we even tell each other about our sex lives! Everyone's relationship with their mother is different and I'm not encouraging you to talk to your mam about your favourite sex position, but what I am saying is that it was when my mam and I talked honestly and openly, our relationship became unbreakable; it deepened, and became equally valuable to both of us. She says the same. It means so much to my mam that I can talk to her when I'm overwhelmed, or I'm struggling with a decision, or I miss Paul. And similarly, when she confides in me, our bond strengthens. We lost my grandma Mavis, her mam, in 2018. She was the matriarch of our family and a hugely positive influence on us all. A little while ago, in 2021, we sold my grandma's house and we all got a bit of inheritance money, and obviously we'd all rather have her, but when my mam rang to tell me the news and got upset, I could console her. Although it was bittersweet, it feels lovely I'm able to be there for her now, to make up for all the times I wasn't there before, and to repay the times she's been there for me.

I recognised recently my relationship with my

mum is beautiful because we're equals. We do everything together – we go to yoga together, we go to bootcamps, she helps me with my work life and to generally just be a better person. And I like to think it's a two-way street now, that we're a good influence on each other. I help her with her Reels for Instagram (super important) and with her new relationship. In almost every aspect of life my mam has more experience than me – she does have thirty years on me after all! – but she met my dad when she was eleven years old and she only ever had eyes for him. Until their marriage ended a few years ago, that was still the case. No points for guessing where I get my loyalty from then, folks, is there? Now I'm the total opposite of my mam – I didn't settle down early (not for lack of trying, mind you!) and I've not had the best luck in the love department, so I've had my fair share of boyfriends and got more experience than her on the man front. Now she's working on her love life, I give her advice and can be a shoulder to cry on if she ever needs it. Our dynamic is different and I know it will always evolve, but I'm so glad we've ended up where we have. We have a relationship filled with balance, respect and trust – I mean, don't get me wrong, we still get on each other's tits at times, but what mother and daughter don't?

## Like fathers, like daughters

One of my earliest memories, when I was about nine or ten, was walking my dad home from my aunt and uncle's house when he was absolutely mortal. He used to sing this song when he'd been drinking, called 'Walking to New Orleans', and on this occasion, he could barely walk home, let alone get to fucking New Orleans. We were getting nowhere, and my mam had gone ahead with Laura in the buggy. She couldn't be arsed with him anymore, and he was using me as a kind of human walking stick. I remember thinking *if this is what drinking looks like, I will never drink. My dad looks like a knob.* Okay, so I probably wasn't using the word 'knob' then, but I knew he was out of control, and could recognise he was relying on a small child to help him walk. I remember even then, when I was so young, that I didn't want to be like him. So it's especially weird to me that that's exactly what happened.

Sometimes I wonder if there's an element of alcoholism that is genetic. I think my DNA played a part, but maybe that's just something I want to believe so I don't have to take ownership of the decisions I've made. I also believe it was a bit of a self-fulfilling prophecy. I was told so many times by family and friends that I was my dad's daughter, and I was inevitably going to end up the same way, so why fight it?

If I'd continued along the path I was on, abusing

alcohol, I would have ended up more like my dad than I would have liked. Because once upon a time, my alcohol use was so out of control. I used it to self-medicate. I used it to mask my insecurities. I used it to quell my feelings of incredible powerlessness. But it doesn't really help with those deeper issues; it can actually make them worse, which is why I have a cautious respect for alcohol now, and acknowledge what it can do to someone.

If I ever have kids, I want a future with them. I want us to have a great relationship, not one littered with unnecessarily painful memories and sadness. I also want to get married and I don't want to be a burden and let down the people who love me, like my dad did to my mam. I want a successful career that spans over decades. I don't want to have to abandon doing what I love because of all-consuming addiction.

Alcohol is a known depressant. Just as I believe healthy exercise is the most under-used antidepressant, alcohol is the most over-used depressant. I've learnt this the hard way. Because it's legal and socially acceptable, we're often in denial about the negative ramifications it's going to have on our mental and physical health. I like to think that drinking too much is totally behind me now because I know it's a recipe for anxiety, and I hate when you get those patches of black where you don't remember things – that just makes me scared. Drinking booze can still be fun and social, but if it starts slipping into other areas of your life and damaging it, I urge you to consider your choices.

It sounds so obvious, but we often forget about it. For me, having a few cocktails with friends, or having a bottle of champagne to celebrate something special, or having a couple of glasses of wine with your boyfriend over dinner is fun and I honestly believe such an important part of my social life and how I enjoy myself, so I'm never going to be a teetotaller. But I've had to develop a way to make alcohol a part of my life without it encroaching negatively onto other areas of it. I'm no longer letting it stop me from enjoying the other things I have worked to achieve.

You shouldn't be drinking so much that it's debilitating, and you're racked with such guilt for the rest of the week that you can't face people or get anything done. Look, once in a while I will still have at it – and listen, my mum is sixty years old and she still has an occasional blinder. I definitely can't judge anyone for choosing to drink large amounts – but it comes back to knowing what you can handle and finding the right balance. Like anything in your life, whether it's having a boyfriend, eating food or having a drink, it should enrich your life, make it better. If you ever find you have more nights crying on the sofa than you do snuggled up in bed with your partner, or if you have more nights worried about how you look than being really proud of your curves, or if you have more nights filled with alcohol-induced fear, anxiety or sadness rather than living in the moment, laughing and building great memories, it's time to make a change.

Given my dad's illness, I have even more knowledge about the downsides and I'd love to know how other daughters and sons of alcoholics have built their own relationship with alcohol, because I know I've found it difficult. It took me realising what I was losing and who I was becoming to finally change my behaviour. I was losing sleep, I was losing friends, I was hating myself, and it dawned on me that I didn't know many nice drunks. We're all fine after a couple of glasses of wine – we're giggly, and funny, and the life and soul of the party – but when people are *drunk* drunk, it's not nice. And I was one of them. We get sloppy, and we get aggressive, and we get clumsy. I don't know anyone who is really lovely when they're absolutely smashed. And I will go on the record and admit I am one of the worst drunks ever. I am all of the things I just mentioned at the same time, plus super obnoxious in this loud, often abrasive, Geordie package. It's just awful for anyone around me. And I got sick of waking up and not remembering who I'd upset, or what I'd done, or where I'd been.

I saw what my dad's addiction did to him physically too, and it was heartbreaking to watch. My dad has had two heart attacks and a stroke, he's got cirrhosis of the liver, and although it hasn't been confirmed that it's linked to alcoholism, he is recovering from cancer of the mouth. We've tried everything with my dad; he's been into rehab, AA meetings and various facilities and we've had him in therapy. I thought the cancer would be the wakeup call he needed, and for a while he really did try and get a handle on it – but sadly the disease normally wins. When he stopped drinking because of his radiotherapy treatment, I felt like I'd got my dad back, because he could listen to me and Laura, and he wasn't this half-version of himself, trying (and failing) to hide his drunkenness or being deathly hungover. He was that clever, funny man that I remembered from my youth.

Unfortunately, once my dad was in remission all of his old bad habits crept back in again – as they have a tendency to – and he's currently working really hard to get things under control again. He says he'll always be an alcoholic, just sometimes he is drinking and sometimes he isn't. He will however always have the desire to drink and sadly I think that's true of all alcoholics.

In the last few years, my dad and his illness have played a huge part in the better decisions I have made around alcohol. Choosing to leave *Geordie Shore*, who I choose to surround myself with, and my choice in men. I always used to want a party boy, I used to think *he'd better be able to keep up with me when I'm out on the lash*, and now as I read back that statement I completely cringe! That shouldn't have entered into my decision-making process about who I was going to date at all. I've now realised that if someone has the same bad habits as you, especially if it's things like drinking too much and partying hard, it becomes toxic very quickly. And that is precisely what happened with quite a few of my exes.

These days, I love a couple of glasses of wine with a nice meal, and I'll probably still whinge the next day on my Insta story and insist I'm hungover, but that's only because I am a total fanny. How I enjoy myself has completely changed now I'm in my thirties. I want more out of my life than being out drunk partying all night, then drawing my curtains and hating myself all of the next day.

It took me a while to get to this point, but seeing my dad's struggles has made me absolutely resolute that I will not be a prisoner to alcohol. The scariest thing is, I know I have it in me, which is really painful for me to admit, because no one ever wants to own up to their weaknesses. But yes, I am predisposed to any type of addiction. If I was going to work out, I had to work out all the time. If I was going to lose weight, I had to meticulously count how many blueberries were on my porridge. And if I was going to party, I was going to be the last one standing. It's taken me a long time to learn about moderation. But watching my dad, and how his illness, his addiction and even in some cases his decisions have affected not only him, but my family, has given me an insight and clarity into what I want my life to be – and more importantly, what I don't want it to be.

I wish I could have learnt another way, and I wish my dad wasn't sick, but that's what life has given me. That ten-year-old girl that said she was never going to drink? I woefully let her down. I abused alcohol all through my teens and twenties, and it's only now, since turning thirty, that I've truly chosen to understand the bad decisions I was making and the path I was on. I've chosen myself. I've chosen to live. I don't want to have a life littered with illness and health issues, and I don't want to make my family worried and sad. I promise myself most days that I won't end up like my dad – and I know there's more to addiction and alcoholism than that – but if willpower, strength and a desire to be more have anything to do with it, I know, in this respect at least, I will not be my father's daughter.

Despite my dad's illness I love him dearly, and I know that for those of you without alcoholic parents that might be a difficult thing for you to comprehend. He has put me and my family through an awful lot and there are some of my childhood memories that I'd rather forget, but my relationship with my dad has taught me one of life's more valuable lessons. My dad's disease taught me that sometimes the people you love aren't who you want them to be, but you just have to love them anyway. And I do.

## Happily unmarried

My mam met my dad when she spotted him through the school gates, when she was about eleven years old. Before she'd even spoken to him, she'd decided he was the one for her. You've got to hand it to me mam. She's a determined woman and when she decides she wants something, more often than not she gets it. I mean, my dad loved her too – and how could he not? Small, petite, blonde, and full of fun – what's not to love? My dad on the other hand was shy, more subdued, but still liked a party and had loads of great friends. He was also very tall and handsome. They were the perfect couple as far as everyone was concerned. They started going out at fifteen, were engaged at nineteen, married at twenty-four, had me at twenty-nine and Laura at thirty-three ... it's the stuff that fairytales are made of.

But sadly, this is real life, not a storybook, and things don't always work out the way you want them to. I'll just tell you, this is the first time throughout this whole book-writing process I've felt uncomfortable. And it's not because it's painful for me – there have been plenty other memories that have been difficult to recall which have taken me back to times I'd rather forget. No, this is because it's really not my story to tell, it's theirs, and even though I'm their daughter, only my mam and dad can really know what happened between them.

I do however think it's safe to say my dad's alcoholism played a huge role in the demise of their happy marriage. His illness made it very difficult for them to live a normal and happy life, no matter how hard my mam tried.

But I think, as well, who they were as people changed. They were no longer the same eleven-year-olds who kissed through the fence: they'd grown up and just weren't the same. My mam is adventurous and driven, wants to see the whole world, go to every party and live her life to the fullest. Whereas my dad is a lot more content to be closer to home, hates flying, loves his sofa and his documentaries and a much slower, although nonetheless fulfilling, way of life. It makes me think that even if my dad hadn't been so poorly and made their marriage very strained the outcome would have been the same.

I don't think it matters when your parents separate, whether you're four years old or forty-four years old, you still kind of want them to stay together, don't ya. But my parents have been apart for about six years now and I can honestly say, even though it was hard for us all, they did the right thing. I want everyone I care about to be in loving relationships with partners who they consider to be their equal, and I want them to do the things that make them happy. And I can see that the people my parents have ended up with suit them, the people they've become. And they all seem really happy. Which is all I have ever wanted for them.

They still have a lot of love and respect for each other too and I think that's been imperative in keeping our family as close as we all are. They've been really mature and dignified throughout it all – even though I know it can't have been easy to move on from the only person they'd ever loved at the time. But their separation taught me a lot, and I'll forever be grateful to my mam and dad for a lot of things. That doesn't change just because they're not together anymore, and I think we need to understand that. Parents have every right to happiness, to love, to start over again, to get back out there and find the happily-ever-after they deserve. I would hate my parents to have stayed unhappily married to protect my feelings. Because I still have two parents, even though they aren't married anymore.

I would encourage you all to extend the same level of understanding to your parents if they're going through something similar. Because they're more than just your mam and dad and they do not exist just to serve your narrative – they need their own lives and happiness too.

## Sister, sister

Me and my sister Laura's relationship hasn't been an easy ride either. We are such wildly different people. She's three and a half years younger than me, so when we were kids we had periods where we'd almost be getting on, and then we'd fight like cat and dog – I mean physically fight. I remember once she wanted a go on the dance mat, and I wouldn't let her on it because I was such a cow when I was fifteen, and she literally went for me. My mam and dad were in the kitchen and my mam wanted to get involved, but my dad said, 'Stand back, Caroll – you don't want to get involved with that,' while Laura was whacking my head on the kitchen bench. Complete and utter savages. But I think fighting, arguing, periods of closeness – they're all part and parcel of having a sibling.

We had wild times, and our path to being as close as we are now wasn't smooth – but I don't think it ever does run smoothly with sisters. We're not so close in age that we were fighting over the same boy, and we've always had different taste in men anyway. I like blokes almost prettier than me and Laura prefers a more rugged gentleman caller. It was more like the usual, petty squabbles that sisters have over clothes and which member of Boyzone is fitter or which Britney song is better. But once we grew up, it got a lot better. At school she had to deal with all the 'Oh, you're Vicky Pattison's sister' shite that teachers do when they've taught your brother or sister before you, and she didn't really get to establish her own identity. She was quite a tearaway, super cool and rebellious, whereas I was a real swot and I don't think she liked it – indeed, it didn't do our relationship any favours. Once I went off to university our relationship flourished, while I was away she grew into this really self-assured person, very independent and strong, and I just felt really lucky to call her my sister I suppose. She was really funny and she didn't stand for anyone's shit, and I had a lot of time for her.

Now I look at her in awe. She works two jobs, is a wife and a mother, helps me look after my money, and is always on the phone to me if someone is mean to me on the internet, despite having so much going on in her own life. Yes, we have ups and downs, anyone with a sibling knows it's never straightforward, but we own our differences, which has helped our bond work. She's not trying to come for anything that's mine and I'm not trying to come for anything that's hers! When I did *I'm a Celeb*, I was allowed to take two people to Australia, and my dad was so unwell he couldn't really travel, so I'd have instantly chosen Laura and my mam, but Laura said 'I can't imagine anything worse!' I thought, *are you mad? An all-expenses-paid trip to Australia, to live in the Versace Hotel for three weeks while I get eaten alive by bugs and chew on kangaroo balls,* but she said, 'I don't want to go on the long plane journey, I don't want to have to talk to loads of people I don't know, and if they want me to be on telly, they can fuck off.' That's her mentality, and all she's ever wanted to be is a mam, and while I can't relate to that, I can respect it.

I don't know if I'll ever be a mother, but for Laura it's been a burning desire of hers forever. Our relationship has changed now she has kids – it's amazing how things grow and develop. She's seen me at my lowest, and I've seen her when things are bad, too. We have no secrets. When you do have that closeness and transparency, you can properly be there for each other, and because we are so different, we're able to be so happy for each other without any flickers of jealousy, or coveting each other's lifestyle. We're fiercely protective of each other – I can't tell you how many boyfriends of hers I've threatened and absolutely meant it as well. 'If you hurt her, I will absolutely burn your life to the ground,' I'd tell these massive rugby players she dated. Laura finds it hilarious when anyone is scared of me because I'm all of five foot six and 120 lb, but if she threatens my fellas, it's a whole other story, because she's proper scary. Everybody is scared of Laura. Laura also controls my money – not because I'm frivolous (in fact, I'm the polar opposite, I'm frugal if anything) but because I'm dopey. I've had a lot of people take advantage of me over the years and I'm a bit of a bleeding heart. Laura on the other hand isn't stupid when it comes to money and you'd have to get up pretty early in the morning to pull the wool over her eyes. She's savvier than me, and not as much of a fanny. I need someone like her in my corner. In fact, I'd go as far to say that everyone needs a 'Laura' in their corner.

# The Secret To... finding peace within your family

* Family relationships can change, evolve, grow. Don't bring all your old feelings and judgements to every new situation or new argument. Actively work at seeing things how they stand currently, without preconceived ideas. This will allow you a fresh start when things have got a bit fraught.

* Your family should have your back – but that doesn't mean they can't give you feedback when they think you're making mistakes or could do better. Your parents, grandparents and siblings should be your biggest fans but also your kindest critics, and you should be the same to them. They don't have to blindly tell you you're right when you could do with some sound advice from people who genuinely care. Sycophants are no help to anyone.

* There is no place for jealousy within a family. Celebrate your differences rather than comparing everything you have, do and are. Power struggles rarely work out well. Balance, respect and trust are a good groundwork to family life.

You will get on each other's tits at times. That's
normal. Look at the bigger picture.

* Your parents are their own people with their own
  dreams and goals. They don't simply exist to
  cater to your every whim. Imagine your parents
  as children, teenagers or at the age you are now.
  It will humanise them, and allow you to forge a
  more equal relationship.

* Family is what you make it from what you've
  been given. You can't make a silk purse out of
  a sow's ear. Sometimes relationships with relatives don't work, or they are unhealthy, despite
  the shared DNA. Give it your best, but don't
  become a punching bag. If you have to let go of
  toxic relationships for your mental health, allow
  yourself to, and build a family from friends who
  do love and care for you. Family has very little
  to do with blood and a whole heap to do with
  who told you they loved you and proved it –
  remember that.

## PREPARE YOUR PURPOSE

If you want a healthy family dynamic, you can't go straight to blame when things don't go your way. Look at your own actions and attitude. I used to think about my family in relation to me, especially my mam – forgetting she was her own person. We can be quite self-absorbed, especially when we're young. So when issues or niggles arise, don't point fingers without first looking inwards. If you ask yourself questions before you condemn your family, you might get some clarity, feelings potentially won't get hurt and relationships may be saved and turned into healthier, happier ones. Which is what we all want really, isn't it? Think about a recent argument or disagreement you had with your family – or even just a situation that's left a bad taste in your mouth. Grab a pen and jot down your answers to the questions below.

Write down what happened.

_____

_____

_____

_____

_____

How did you express how you were feeling? Did you shout or lose your temper?

_____

_____

_____

_____

In retrospect, do you feel you handled the situation the best you could have? Were you proud of how you dealt with it? Did you get the outcome you wanted?

_____

_____

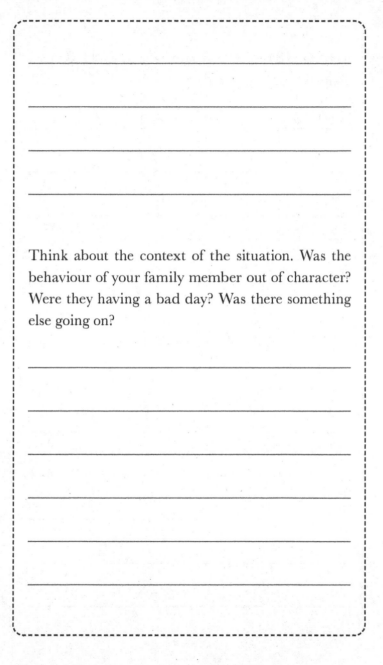

_____

_____

_____

_____

Think about the context of the situation. Was the behaviour of your family member out of character? Were they having a bad day? Was there something else going on?

_____

_____

_____

_____

_____

_____

Having had time to re-evaluate, how could you have handled the situation better?

_____

_____

_____

_____

_____

_____

_____

_____

_____

_____

_____

# 5

# Life after heartbreak

*Don't let a bad chapter in your life define your entire story*

We accept the love we think we deserve. That is what I truly believe when it comes to romantic relationships. Beyond that, you accept the love you've observed at home, as a child. This is a hard thing for me to admit because I love my dad and he has been a good dad to me over the years and always loved us to the best of his ability, and saying anything negative about him is difficult. But I can't get away from the truth that my mam gave everything to him and their marriage, and ultimately, he couldn't improve for her, and he couldn't get better for us. As a kid, however much your parents think they shield you and they're protecting you from the worst of it, children are intuitive, they can read energies and they pick up on even the smallest things, and they see so much more than you know. I knew as a child that there was something wrong, and I watched my mam give every inch of herself to a man that was not getting better – if anything he was getting worse. I just watched as that relationship constantly took from her and drained her . . .

And that's what I thought love was.

That's what I'd seen. A woman fighting hard to make it work, a woman hiding her partner's shortcomings from everyone else however hard things were for her, a woman acting like everything was okay, and I assumed that's what I had to do, too. And subsequently, and this isn't something I did consciously, my pattern became that I fell for broken men. Almost every time. Men with deep, real psychological issues that made them abusive, cruel, addicts, everything unhealthy you can name, that's who I fell for – and I didn't ever make any of them better, they just made me worse. I spent years trying to fix these fellas thinking that's what love was . . . and it left me almost broken.

It's a basic human desire to want to be loved and feel safe, and I'm no different. I've always wanted to be loved so much, and even if I was feeling insecure or having down days, and not feeling like a ten all the time in other areas of my life, I've always been self-assured enough to know what I bring to the table in a relationship – I don't cheat, I don't hurt people intentionally, I respect you if I'm with you, and I definitely don't want to live off you. All in all, I'm a good girlfriend, but still, despite that, for a large chunk of my life I had nothing but heartbreak, and it was such a depressing narrative.

I wanted to be loved so much that I repeatedly fell too hard and too fast for the wrong people. Because I'm confident I thought I needed a typical male – someone who was tall, strong and always the loudest person in the room. It's taken me fifteen years of dating to realise the loudest man in the room is more often than not the most insecure. I fell for these blokes because they were self-assured, thinking *you'll be able to handle me, and handle my mates, my powerful opinions and the fact that I earn my own money.* But they can't. They're silly little boys. All these men I dated had a pattern. Instead of sitting me down and being honest and upfront with me, admitting, 'I feel out of my depth with you. You have shown me that I'm not as successful as I thought. You have shown me that I want more,' or even 'I thought I wanted a successful woman but actually I just want one who will applaud me and tell me I'm perfect all the time,' they couldn't be vulnerable and honest. If they'd said anything like that it would have been far more emotionally evolved than what they actually did, which was try to exert their masculinity in other fucking painful ways. These men feel validated by cheating on you: if you aren't constantly telling them how amazing they are – how powerful, how sexy – they'll find someone who will. That's how they feel like men again – well at least these boys I picked. Or they hit you. And honestly, having felt the very real pain of both, I still don't know which is worse.

## Queen of Hearts

It was so long ago now, but I had one man who couldn't deal with who I was so he tried to keep me small. He couldn't raise his game so he dragged me down to my lowest level with him. There's that saying: I thought I needed a smaller crown, but actually I just needed a man with bigger hands. It's so true. I used to reduce myself, and not be as outgoing at parties, or not make that joke or be that sparkly version of myself that I loved because it intimidated the men I was dating, which was weird because that's what they liked about me in the first place. But once I was theirs, they wanted me dampened.

Things totally changed with Ercan, my loving boyfriend, who let me be me. He loves that I'm loud, silly and jokey – he's not intimidated at all – he's proud of me! It took meeting him to appreciate what I did and didn't need from a partner. He walks into a room and he doesn't demand attention, he's not big headed, he's super unassuming, and people might not know who he is before he gets there, but by the time he leaves, everyone knows who he is, and everyone likes him. He hasn't bullied people, or intimidated them, or insisted on being the centre of attention, he's just slowly worked his way around the group, introducing himself, being interested in others, being kind. He's quietly confident and so secure in who he is, he allows everyone to be exactly who they are too. I've never met anyone who doesn't like Ercan. And he treats me like a queen. You need to make sure you're with a partner who treats you like royalty, too.

Love is the one thing in life that shouldn't hurt. There is pain everywhere. In work there are setbacks – you don't get the promotion and it hurts. If you want to have a family, childbirth hurts! Even self-improvement can be uncomfortable and painful at times. But love? Nah. Love should be exempt from that. Your partner should be your equal, providing you with solace; they should be a constant that brings you peace, self-acceptance and safety. If they're not doing that, it's not love.

I was convinced I was in love with various men, but I wasn't really, until I met Ercan. With him, I was finally able to sit with someone in baked bean-stained pyjamas, with no makeup on, not having had a shower or brushed my teeth, and have him roll over and give me a kiss, knowing he finds me just as worthy of his devotion as when I'm on a red carpet.

That's true love. So, if you're in a relationship with someone who is making you feel like you're not a queen, or you're not a prize, or not wonderful just as you are, or who is exacerbating your existing insecurities and making you feel like you're not safe, it's not love – it's a game, and it's fucking mean, and it's immature, and it has no place in your life.

## Consent to be content

I'm still learning so much from all the powerful conversations happening around me right now on women's rights and gender equality. I'm looking back on episodes from my life, and I'm realising there were moments when I was manipulated and taken advantage of. I definitely didn't understand the importance of consent. There's one instance that stands out in my head that is super, super troubling, and it's only in later life that I've been able to articulate what happened and the massively damaging effects it had on me as a person. I was on *Geordie Shore* and I hadn't had sex on television. I didn't want to; it wasn't who I was. Anyway, I started going out with another cast member and it became really serious, but I still didn't want to have sex on telly because I didn't want everyone to see me and I knew my mam was watching and I knew it would upset her. But my partner wore me down, constantly badgering me, telling me it would look weird if we didn't have sex because we were a couple, telling me everyone was teasing him because he wasn't having sex with me. And it got to the point I felt so browbeaten, confused and demoralised by his constant demands, the barrage of begging, that I let him. I thought it was something I had to do to keep my boyfriend happy.

But girls – what about your happiness? You shouldn't be made to do anything that makes you uncomfortable. That one act led me to get so much abuse online, while he got nothing. Why? Because I am a woman and he was a man. Again, if the girls are getting criticised, so should the boys! The producers of the show never showed the begging that led to that point to at least have it in context. It ruined my relationship with my mam for ages, my dad couldn't even look at me, and it affected how I saw myself. To this day, I still feel let down that no one stepped in to say that wasn't right, or to tell me I could say no, or advise me to wait until I grew up a bit and had a stronger sense of self. I don't want any girls to be in that position I was in, when they feel they have to silence their better instincts because they think their focus has to be on keeping their partner happy, or to make him stay, or to make him love them more. It's painful and it's wrong.

The first time someone says no they should be

listened to. No means no unequivocally. I don't know why we've taught women they have to be subservient and submissive. Why do we teach women they need to walk home a certain way, or dress a certain way or to act a certain way when really all we should be doing is teaching men how to respect them? Teaching men not to attack us, to make us feel intimidated or to rape us.

## Let's talk about sex

I do feel positive though. I do feel like for the first time ever, mothers, fathers – adults in general – are aware of their responsibility to the next generation and are endeavouring to instill in them principles that will lead to more equality and mutual respect. Girls are being taught how to stand up for themselves, take precautions, to refuse to be pushed into anything that feels wrong, and not to accept the idea that they have to do whatever a man wants to keep him happy or make him stay with you. And likewise, boys are now being taught to respect women, to comprehend that no means no. We are taking huge steps, but this really should have happened decades ago, and even now, not everyone is along for the ride. There is so much work, and so much healing, that still needs to be done.

Sex is a privilege, and something that should be

incredibly special with someone you adore and feel a deep trust with. I was incredibly lucky that the person I lost my virginity to is still one of my good friends now. He's a wonderful man, and whoever ends up with him will be incredibly lucky. He's kind, patient and handsome, and because of all that I have had real faith in men from a young age. That's the type of person you want to give yourself to, and it doesn't matter if you're not with them for the rest of your life. God, that would have made life easier, but things don't often work out like that. You've got lots of living to do, and who cares if you're on your first sexual partner or your tenth, it is always your decision who you get into bed with.

And if someone is rushing or pressurising you, it is wrong; or if you feel like them liking you hinges on you having sex with them, then they don't really like you at all. Respect yourself and have enough faith and self-worth to know you should never feel uncomfortable. A person who loves you will never make you feel uneasy, unsafe or disrespected. If they make you feel like it's a duty, or they're bringing you stress and anxiety, they are not the one for you, please believe me. I wish someone had sat me down and said all this when I was younger, but when I was growing up conversations about sex were still considered incredibly taboo. It was almost as if, when I was growing up, a girl should feel grateful that a boy wanted to have sex with her at all. That is bullshit. Any woman reading this needs to know you are a fucking prize! You are beautiful, you are powerful, you are worthy of love beyond measure – and any man who gets to touch your nunny is lucky, and he'd best act like a king because you are a queen. I get so frustrated thinking about when I was younger, when talking about sex was shameful, and having control over your body just wasn't something that was discussed. Asserting your rights and power and calling yourself a feminist brought a stigma with them ... and the collective subservience that was put upon us as women led me into some heartbreaking situations. If I can help any young woman avoid being in a similar circumstance, I'd consider this entire book a success.

## Bad romance

Eventually I realised I deserved to be loved. There were loads of warning signs in my relationships, I just didn't read them properly, or I chose to ignore them like the stubborn cow I am. For example, when I lost Paul, I couldn't get out of bed for about two weeks; I just couldn't face the world. My fiancé at the time showed me very little sympathy, and if memory serves me correctly, he eventually told me to 'pull yourself together'. And I tried. I believed that was what I should do – that he was right. So I remember going to the gym, and hiding behind a dumbbell rack crying because I wasn't okay, and I wasn't ready to pull myself together. I was lost in grief and should have been allowed to feel that by the person who was supposed to love me most. Someone who truly loved me would have told me I had every right to be broken, I'd just lost one of the most important people in my life. But he just wasn't that guy. Another warning sign was that my friends didn't like him and my sister absolutely hated him. To this day one of pals likes to remind me, 'You know, I never followed him on Instagram. He never sat right with me.' There were many red flags, but in the pursuit of love I continued in our relationship longer than I should have. I couldn't stand the idea of being in the papers again with everyone saying, 'Oh look, Vicky Pattison has driven another one away because she's unlovable, doesn't want kids, is a nightmare to be with, too career focused.' (Choose your favourite, by all means.) 'She can't keep a man!'

I couldn't stand the thought of being seen as a poster girl for heartbreak. So I fought it, and forged forward with something I knew wasn't right, and spent more nights crying on my sister's sofa than being in the house me and my ex shared together. Still, it took him cheating on me and publicly embarrassing me to walk away, because I am loyal to a fault.

I had to be publicly humiliated on a national scale in order to leave him.

That's one of the things I've always said – I understand that relationships break down if you're no longer on the same page, or you've fallen out of love. It's not nice, but it happens, and you have to be honest. I'll get over you falling out of love with me because people change, they grow apart – and also I'm not everyone's cup of tea, which I totally understand. But what I won't get over is being disrespected. Maybe at one point in my life I'd have put up with being disrespected, but I can't anymore. I've spent years trying to be a better role model for young women, and I knew I couldn't let them down. I knew it isn't just about me anymore, and that gives me a huge amount of strength.

Because it's not just me that his disrespect and infidelity damages. It's not just me who's watching, or my family who's watching for my reaction. There are thousands of young girls, and if I stayed with him, I'd be telling all of them it's acceptable not to respect yourself. I've always maintained that – and always thought to myself, *you'd be fucking mad to cheat on me, not because I think I'm some massive prize, or I think you couldn't do better than me, it's because you know I have to do better for women in general.* He could have talked to me, told me the relationship was going too fast, or that he regretted asking me to marry him, or that he'd fallen out of love, but he could not cheat and expect me to stay. I'm just not that girl – I don't believe anyone should be. You deserve so much more. In the past, I have forgiven a lot of things that I shouldn't have. I forgave a partner spending my money, I forgave a partner not coming home because they'd pulled an all-nighter with their lad mates when they promised to come home. I'll work through pretty much anything, but I can't forgive cheating. Even though it was hard to walk away from a house, and the life I had planned out, and a person I'd loved at some point, ultimately I loved myself more. I was at a magical point of recognising my own self-worth, more than I had previously.

When all this happened, and my wedding got cancelled, I was balls deep in the middle of filming a reality show about it. I was contracted up to the eyeballs to film this bloody wedding show, and we all knew we had to pull something out of the bag or risk letting down the network and the production company. So, it got turned into this fly-on-the-wall style show following the breakdown of my relationship and how I put myself back together – *The Break-Up*. Half of me was like, I'm a fucking human being and I need to grieve, I'm so broken, and the other half of me was like this man has taken the future I had planned for myself, the relationship I thought I wanted, my wedding, he has made me a victim in so many people's eyes. I refuse to let him take my career as well. That's why I did it. You spend years building relationships with networks and production companies – I couldn't throw all that away. And I stand by it, because I showed women that if they're being disrespected, it doesn't matter how far along the line you are, you can walk away and you can survive, and in my case as you can see, you can even thrive!

Now I thank my lucky stars he did what he did. I was unhappy, living a half-life, and deep down I knew he wasn't a nice person. I knew he wouldn't really let me be myself and that he'd try to keep me down. Looking back, there were little things; things I should have been brave enough to stand up to him about. If we were doing a photoshoot together and I'd ask the photographer to take a few more pictures, he'd say things like 'The problem with you is you're not as pretty as you think you are,' which never failed to leave me feeling insecure and unattractive. His favourite line to say whenever I threatened to leave him, telling him I knew I deserved better and this relationship wasn't right, was 'See, you forget, you think you're Vicky who won the jungle, but I know you're Vicky from *Geordie Shore*.' He had a talent for zoning in on insecurities and exploiting them; a master manipulator who distanced me from my friends and family, drip-feeding me things about my mam wanting to be famous and my sister spending my money. He almost got into my head and made me completely dependent on him with nowhere to go.

My experience is common. So many people do this in relationships – and not just men, women too. My advice, which has taken me years to learn, is this: I used to believe love had to hurt – if you're *really* in love it had to physically hurt – and I was conditioned to love the bad boys. If they leave the room, you feel pain and need to ring them every five minutes. But that isn't love, that's insecurity and codependency – you're in a relationship that you don't feel safe in, and it's making you vulnerable. Please see it for what it is: a bad romance. Protect your heart and understand that you deserve a relationship that makes you feel safe, appreciated and loved.

## Timing is everything?

We need to stop the judgement we put on other women about their relationships, and how and when they need to be in one. I hate the notion that anyone going through a break-up needs to give themselves time to recover alone, that there is a set time it takes for a heart to heal. We are all different. Swearing off men and doing sunrise yoga for a year won't make you happy if you don't want to be alone. That might work for some people, but it isn't a prescription we all have to follow; we're all different. Stop making women feel bad for wanting to be loved, or for falling in love fast, and don't make women feel bad for wanting to have a partner. Diminishing the power of a solid partnership is wrong – we should encourage each other to have whatever makes us happy.

I felt judgement when I rolled out of my last toxic relationship, and then after three months on my own met Ercan. Everyone around me was saying 'It's too soon, you need time, you need to heal from the last one' and even though I knew my own mind, I had all that in the back of my head and it made me push him away. I made him suffer because I believed I had to conform to someone else's timeline about when it was the right time for me to fall in love again.

There are certain things in life that you can't plan for. You can't protect yourself from a broken heart, unfortunately, but on the flipside, you can't plan when you fall in love either. That's the pleasure and pain of romance, I'm afraid. I did not envisage myself being thirty-one and single. I was supposed to be married, maybe even be a mother, by then and of course it didn't quite work out like that. So, when I met Ercan and finally seemed to be happy again you'd think everyone would just be ecstatic that I wasn't sporadically bursting into tears and periodically stalking my ex's Instagram every time I'd had a gin. But no, everyone had an opinion all right – it just wasn't one I wanted to hear. If I'd listened to everyone's well-intentioned but completely misguided blah blah blahs, about moving on too soon, I would have missed out on the person who is my forever person, and I get mad at that. I get angry when people try to impose their views and say there is a right or wrong way to do love. There isn't – it is your heart, and only you know it. What would I have lost if Ercan wasn't the one? I'd already had partners who cheated on me, who stole my money, who abused me emotionally. What good would have come from me not taking this new chance? There's more to lose if you don't take those risks. I don't want anyone to be in pain, and I don't wish the things I've gone through on any woman, but it can happen to anyone. And when it does you pick yourself up, and eventually you will find the right one – but only if you get yourself back out there.

I always say, we all make mistakes, that's human, just don't make the same ones over and over. But I did. Oh god, did I ever! I kept repeating the same mistakes. When it came to men, I'd fall for supposedly very secure, arrogant, pretty boys, time after time. That's what frustrated me looking back. Don't get me wrong, I will gladly make a new mistake every single day of my life – that's how you grow, that's how you learn – but when you keep making the same mistake it doesn't show growth, it shows ignorance – and

I'm annoyed that when I came to my love life I did just that. More than once. I found myself in a painful cycle of heartbreak and pain with fellas that were just so wrong for me.

## Nobody's perfect

No relationship is perfect. I think an important part of growing up and allowing yourself to fall in love with the right person is accepting this and managing your expectations. When I was eighteen years old and looking for a boyfriend, I had a list as long as my arm: must look like Ryan Gosling, be incredibly witty, as smart as a dart, huge schlong – all these things. A man had to be everything! As you can tell from that list, I was incredibly fussy and picky . . . and yet I still ended up going out with utter scumbags! As you get older you realise a list is nice, and it's good to have standards, but it doesn't matter what colour his hair is – it's how he makes you feel. Kindness is key. Little acts of thoughtfulness and generosity every day can go a long way, whether it's little treats to find in the fridge, remembering how they like the bed made, sending them a newspaper article you think they'd find interesting . . . remind each other when you can that you're special to each other.

How a man made me feel wasn't even on my radar

when I was younger. I'd worry too much about how I made *him* feel, and my mates would have been more interested to know how big his dick was. But as I've got older, I've realised what I thought was important really isn't. Does Ercan make me happy? Yes, he does. Does he make me happy every single second of every single day? No! That would be madness! Nobody is happy all the time, nobody likes the person they're going out with twenty-four hours a day, seven days a week, twelve months of the year, but do you love them all the time? Sometimes Ercan gets on my tits. Sometimes I think if I have to pick up another one of his socks, I'm going to lose my shit. Just recently, Ercan took my keys by mistake, which made me late for a really important audition I was already super nervous about. I kept saying to him on the phone, while I was searching the house, 'Do you have them?' and he insisted he didn't. Anyway, at the end of the day when I was back home again, he called me, and started being *way* too sweet considering I'd been rude to him on the phone about the keys, saying 'I've missed you so much today' blah blah, and I thought, *hmm, I smell a rat.*

'Why are you being so nice to me?' I demanded.

'Don't be mad,' he confessed after a brief silence, 'but I've got your keys in the car.'

Well, naturally I wanted to string him up; I hated him so much in that moment, but I still loved him.

There is no point in sitting and seething – it doesn't help anyone. So I accepted his apology and moved on. And do I honestly think he looks at me every day and thinks I'm perfect? No! Of course not. He thinks my voice is too loud and my laugh is a bit annoying. It was a good reminder that no relationship and no person is perfect. We're all a little bit crazy, so you just have to find the person who can handle your crazy and vice versa. No relationship is constant sunshine, but when two people share one umbrella, you can survive the storm together.

## My Happily Ever After

I'm very thankful for what I've found in Ercan. I realised on our first date that he was different to the other men I'd dated up till then. How we met is not as romantic a story as I'd like it to be, but that's life. I had a *really* romantic story with my ex and we all saw how that worked out, so maybe the meet-cute moment isn't important. I'd been following Ercan on Instagram for years, but I can't remember why or how. He must have just popped up on my explore page and because – let's get this right – he is a lovely bit of kit and I am only human, I followed him. I remember he'd posted a topless picture, and I had no idea who he was but I thought, *what a beautiful human,*

*FOLLOW!* I was single at the time and didn't think any more of it. Not long after doing so, I met my ex, so I never chatted to Ercan, and that was that.

Next, he says – this is his version and he's probably right, because when I broke up with my ex I did go on a whole, typical single-girl rampage, posting attention-seeking selfies and looking at cute boys – I liked a picture of his, and he thought to himself, *that's weird, I thought she had a fella?* He went on my page, checked through all my photos, and couldn't find any of my ex – no sign of the bloke – because I'd deleted them all when I was angry and hurt, and he realised I was single.

Soon after, I was out for the night with my mate Gav and he took a really good photo of me, so I put it up, and Ercan slid into my DMs with lots of clapping emojis. The rest is, as they say, history. Even though our first interactions were across social media, pretty superficial and generic, I just knew there was something different about him when we began talking. After I broke up with my ex, lots of people messaged me. It was a very public break-up and I was single girl number one again. There's no other way to put it than this: my DMs were lit! I was in demand, hot property. But Ercan was the only one who messaged me that I actually wanted to go on a date with.

Actually that date nearly didn't happen because of my nerves. I was filming a show – my break-up show that had been a wedding show – and I remember talking to my friend Pete a few hours before me and Ercan were supposed to meet.

'I don't know if I'll go, I'm nervous,' I said, showing him a photo.

'I know this fella,' he exclaimed. 'He was on *TOWIE*.'

'Fuck off!' I said, my heart dropping. The last thing I wanted, rolling off the back of another public break-up, was a relationship with someone in the public eye. I started to panic and thoughts of cancelling the date swirled in my mind. For anyone who doesn't know, by the way, Pete was totally right – Ercan had been on *TOWIE*. But only for about five minutes, and if you'd blinked you would have missed him. Ercan is too nice, you see, too kind for reality television really. I think you've got to have a little bit of sass or edge, and poor Ercan is devoid of edge. In the nicest possible way, he's a circle. And I love him for that. I've got enough edge for the both of us anyway. I'd been interested in dating him because I thought he worked on a building site. He seemed handsome, normal, nice. I thought he'd give me structure – he'd worked as a builder after all – and be the opposite of anyone I'd ever dated before. And now, here I am, just a couple hours from a first date with another reality TV person! Argh! I'm not going, I decided.

I went back to my makeup artist's house and said,

'I'm not going to go! He's on *TOWIE* and Pete says I'm taller than him!'

'Take a breather!' she advised. 'Who cares if he was on *TOWIE*, and who cares how tall he is? You have to start moving on, I can't watch you cry anymore. What happens if it doesn't go well and you don't like him? So what? You've got to get yourself out there and try something new. What's the alternative? You sit in a hotel room and cry again. On your own.'

I knew she was right. Even if it didn't go well, and I ended the night crying in a hotel room – nothing ventured, nothing gained. So I went, after sending him some pretty weird messages all day, warning him that filming might run over, that we might have to cancel or postpone, setting him up to be let down. He must have thought I was absolutely crackers.

But I got there in the end. He arrived at my hotel in London and he was so handsome in real life that I swear I became nervous all over again. I've never been the type of girl who is nervous around boys – either they like me and that's great, or they don't and I will survive. Obviously, I was vulnerable, straight after having the worst confidence knock ever, so when he turned up and he was every inch the Turkish-Cypriot god that he is, I completely lost my head. I became mute, probably for the first time in my life, and as we all know I'm a complete gobshite normally.

'I thought we'd go to Nobu,' he said, and I loved

that – a man taking charge. And he was taller than me, so suck that, Pete! He had a Gucci scarf and a smart overcoat, and he'd obviously put so much thought into his outfit, which made me feel warm and fuzzy.

By the time we got to Nobu, a beautiful Japanese restaurant in Mayfair, I'd calmed down a bit and found my voice. I was still nervous, but we had a couple of drinks which helped. He's only just admitted in the last year that he was so nervous he'd gone for some drinks with his mates beforehand. And I remember holding his hand and thinking *that's a really sweaty hand*, and now I know it was because he was a bit tipsy. I couldn't tell at the time – on the surface he was as cool as a cucumber in a bowler hat. He was wonderful.

I remember this one point when we were talking about him liking my picture, and him thinking I had a fella. I said I didn't really want to talk about it, but that relationship hadn't turned out the way I thought it would, that my ex wasn't the person I thought he was, and that I'd had a hard couple of months, but things were looking up and here I was now. I was trying so hard not to cry – I can still cry now about what my ex did to me and it doesn't mean that I still love him, just that it had a profound effect on who I am – but I was visibly tearful and he just reached across the table and held my hand. It was such a simple gesture, but given the last couple of months had been so difficult and he was a relative stranger, it meant so much . . . and before I knew it, I was necking on with him in Nobu, wasn't I?

The big difference between Ercan and the other men I dated is me and my attitude to what I want and need. I used to think I needed a man who had his whole life figured out. Because I was successful professionally, I thought I needed to be with someone who matched that. But that doesn't matter at all. Ercan is considerably younger than me, he's twenty-seven and still working out who he is, like I was when I was his age. I never needed anyone else's money, but I thought I needed someone who had their own money, career and success so they wouldn't find me intimidating. But that's bullshit. What I actually need, what we all need, is someone who is secure in who they are. Ercan openly admits that he's studying to become a personal trainer, so is working in his friend's shop until he's totally qualified and can do something he's passionate about. He's a nice man, has a lovely family, is kind to me. And it doesn't hurt that he's incredibly easy on the eye.

I worked out that with all of my exes, there was a kind of competition – especially when I went out with boys who were also in the public eye and doing similar things to me. They could never cope with letting me have some of the limelight, or worse, that I was busier or more successful than them. It's not that I am desperate for fame – if I could find another way to make the money I do out of the public eye, I would definitely do it. Fame is so invasive, and it's difficult to be what everybody wants you to be all the time. If I could be super creative and successful behind the scenes so I could still go out and get drunk and look like a butthole, I'd love that. But that's not the life I've got right now, and instead of being envious or competitive, Ercan is very supportive of what I do. And proud! I think that's what I've been missing.

## Keep your eyes on the prize

I know my worth now and that is a huge part of why my current relationship works. A man will not make you happy; you have to be happy with who you are in yourself and then a nice relationship will add to that. It will not solve all your problems – that's down to you. I can slag off exes till the cows come home but I don't know if anyone would have made me happy before, because I had my own demons, and I had my own things I had to get through. Two years ago, when I was thirty-one, after so much shit, so much heartache, so much pain, so much growth, I was ready to be loved. I'd been through a lot, proved to myself I could survive and I wasn't afraid of love or dating anymore. I wasn't afraid of getting my heart broken, or seeing my boyfriend kiss someone else, or losing my pride, because I'd been there and done that and knew I could live through it. I think it was always going to take a remarkable man to make me fall in love, and accept I was a remarkable woman, too.

And so are you all. Once you realise you owe yourself love and acceptance, and that you're capable of brilliant things, and you own your power, things will fall into place – and you don't have to take my word for it! It's probably happened to loads of you reading this right now, and you'll be nodding your head, knowing I'm right. For those of you it hasn't happened to yet, have patience. Or if you don't feel the need for a partner, you do you. Everything will be alright in the end – and if it's not alright, it's not the end. You don't need to be in a relationship to be happy. You can find love everywhere. That's what I believe about love. Don't settle for people who make you sad. Don't listen to people telling you what's right and wrong, find out what works for you and run with that. Broaden your horizons. Date outside your 'type', don't, don't be in a rush and don't settle for any less than you deserve. Oh, and don't forget to have fun! You're a prize, and the person who wins your heart will be very, very lucky.

## The Secret To... lasting love

The path of true love never did run smooth. Help yourself stay content and balanced in your relationship by remembering a few reasons you need to value your partner – and yourself!

* Put each other on a pedestal. Acknowledge you're both lucky. Don't allow yourself to feel lesser, or make your partner feel insecure because you are feeling insecure. And match energies always – it's so important in a relationship that you feel like someone else is giving as much effort as you are. The alternative just leads to resentment and arguments.

* Use little acts of kindness every day: listen to your partner's stories (without scrolling through Instagram while they're talking), leave romantic notes with their lunch, ask how their day was, and make sure you never stop kissing each other hello and goodbye. The little, simple things keep the big magic going.

* Speak up for yourself. Don't sit and seethe, ask for what you need, and if the shoe is on the other

foot, respond well – don't just kick off. If your partner starts a conversation with you about changes they need, be measured and open. Clear communication is key for a healthy relationship, and although hearing things about yourself that you don't want to hear is never nice, try not to be defensive. We can all be better partners and the only way to achieve that is through open channels of communication and understanding.

* Keep out the negative influencers. Safeguard your relationship from people whose opinions are not wanted: those who may be envious, or who ridicule your loved-up state of mind. Pay attention to how you feel – head, heart and gut – more than paying attention to what everyone else says.

* Never forget why you fell in love with that person. It's so easy – when you're busy or life gets in the way and your and your partner's schedules conflict – to not truly see them. Always make time for each other and remember why they became so special to you in the first place – we can sometimes take the people closest to us for granted when we're rushing through life, and that is a guaranteed way to end up unhappy or alone.

✴ This sounds really silly, but I swear it's important: compliment your partner. That feeling you
   get when someone tells you you're beautiful, or
   funny, or a great mam – it's magic. And you have
   the power to make the person you love light up
   with your kind words. So do it. Sprinkle those
   compliments everywhere like kind confetti and
   watch your partner bloom, grow and sparkle in
   your presence.

✴ If you do find yourself single for a time, try and
   enjoy that period of your life while it lasts. I used
   to throw myself into work – doing *MasterChef,*
   *Coach Trip* and filming my own reality show in
   the space of six months. It was a lot, but it was
   the perfect distraction from my love life, and it
   reminded me what I was capable of *outside* of just
   being a girlfriend, fiancée or wife. I loved my job;
   travelling and meeting new people and working
   on my career proved I was strong and capable.
   So, if you find yourself single, use the time to
   focus on you and what you want. Don't wallow.
   Build up your confidence by fucking getting out
   there and reminding yourself what you're good
   at . . . you are a powerful, bad bitch!

## PREPARE YOUR PURPOSE

Have a serious think about the relationship you're in right now, or the partner you're coveting. Look at these questions, and circle yes or no. Hopefully, they'll really help you decipher if this is a good enough person for you to invest your time in:

| | | |
|---|---|---|
| Do you know, when they go on a night out, that you've got nothing to worry about? | Yes | No |
| Do you miss them when you've spent time apart? | Yes | No |
| Do they make you a better person? | Yes | No |
| Have other people noticed you're happier when you're with them? | Yes | No |
| Do your mates and your mam like them? | Yes | No |
| Do you listen to each other attentively, and feel better after talking an issue out? | Yes | No |

| | |
|---|---|
| Can you let your guard down, be your true self comfortably, without fear of criticism or rejection? | Yes    No |
| Overall, do they add more to your day- to- day life than they take away? | Yes    No |
| Do you see yourself together in the future? | Yes    No |
| Do you feel you both are supportive of each other's personal and professional goals? | Yes    No |
| If you could end the relationship, without any of the stress that comes with breaking up, would you? | Yes    No |

# 6

# Looking after your mental wellbeing

*The future is anxiety; the past is regret;*
*but the here and now is hope*

I live with hope. That's all we've got. Hope. Every day I wake up and I hope I can be the best version of me, with the aim of being kind, positive and respectful – and all the rest of that good stuff – to the people I meet! I try not to fixate too much on the past, because it's gone, and I try not to worry too much about the future, because it's uncertain. I grab the day I'm living with both hands, and every day that I *am* kind, positive and respectful, I am moving further and further away from that girl who I hated: the girl who stopped me sleeping at night; the girl who only brought me pain and hurt; the girl who often didn't recognise what she needed to do to maintain good mental health. Over the last decade I have struggled with depression, anxiety and insomnia; I've fought addictive tendencies to exercise and alcohol; and I've come to terms with living a life with guilt and a myriad of sensitivities. Far from dismissing all these issues as weaknesses or failings, I can now look at them as lessons learnt, trials to help me grow as a human being and stories I get to share with others so they don't feel alone. As I talk you through these different, difficult episodes of my life, my desire is that you feel understood, supported – and I hope, if you are battling any of the mental health issues you read about in this chapter, that I give you that most important thing: hope.

## Feeling depressed

I'm relatively intelligent. Even in my deepest moments of self-loathing, when my inner critic is louder than ever, it is something I've always been able to take solace in and be proud of. However, I've discovered that, along with having many advantages, being intelligent has significant drawbacks for those of us who think too much and ponder the world's problems – mainly its link to a higher incidence of depression and anxiety. I think I'm predisposed to consider every possible outcome of a situation. Here's an example of what it's like living in my brain: most other people wake up in the morning and see the sun is shining and assume it will keep shining all day and it'll be a really good day. Not me. I wake up and see the sun is shining and think, *well, it's shining now, that doesn't mean it's still going to be shining in twenty minutes' time.*

*Anything could happen.* And so on, all day long. I plough through every possible eventuality from the minute I wake up – every thought, or fact, or situation that arrives in my head – until I try to go to sleep at night.

I think if you have a constantly overactive brain, the odds are it's going to sometimes end up in dark places. I have extreme highs, when I'll be happy like no other person, when I know I can enter a room and make someone's day with a conversation, and I know if my friends ever need me to, I can turn their day around. But sadly, what goes up must come down, and I have the lows to match those highs. For years I fought the inevitable downs – I drank to cover them, and I made myself so incredibly busy I had no space for them – but of course that was always just delaying the downs so that when I did finally succumb, they felt monumental. Now I have learnt to embrace the fact that life does ebb and flow, and if I'm going to be lucky enough to have incredible, light, bright moments, there is going to be some shade too. I will allow it now. I don't cover it up.

I haven't had severe, recurring bouts of depression where I have felt suicidal over a long period of time, and I feel so much sympathy for people that do have to deal with that in their lives; it must be heartbreaking to have that black hole there as a constant part of your life. In those moments when I've dealt with depressive episodes, knowing how my mind works, knowing who I am, and learning to stop fighting against it, has been crucial.

I've given up trying to be a warrior 24/7. I've given up trying to be someone who can outsmart depression, because you fucking can't. You can't outsmart your mental health. You have to understand you're at the mercy of it. You have to be kind to your mind and body.

## Counting the days

A huge help for me has been giving each day a number to help me understand the ebbs and flows of my life, and my mental reaction to them. I absolutely cannot take credit for this little technique – it was something that my amazing life coach Bill taught me and I'm sure he wouldn't mind me paying his teachings forward. So, numbering your days works like this: super busy days are a 4, kind of busy days are a 3, normal days are a 2 and chilled days are a 1. I used to believe that all my days had to be 4s if I wanted to be a successful and happy person, but it's actually the complete opposite. You cannot pour from an empty cup. You aren't able to be that bright, powerful, sparky version of you on your 4 days if you haven't allowed yourself some time to rest, recuperate and recharge with some 1 days. Let me explain. If I have an incredibly busy but great day, I'll call it a Number 4 Day. I will have got up early, done a workout, gone to a photoshoot, done a radio interview during my lunch break, then bounced straight from the shoot to an event or a big work dinner, and landed home quite late. It's been a full-on day. Chocker. And I know that potentially the next day I can give myself a Number 3 Day. It doesn't always work like this, mind you, and sometimes I have a real run of 4 days – as I'm sure you busy, working people out there can relate to – and in those cases you just have to roll with the punches and do your best to get some 'you' time in where you can. On Number 3 Days I can go out for a big day of filming and then come straight home. Then there's Number 2 Days, which is maybe podcast, podcast, podcast, all back-to-back, but done remotely without leaving my house and most of the time without wearing a bra! (WINNING.) Then there are Number 1 Days. Those are the days I allow myself to have a lie in, eat custard creams all day, and allow myself to cry a bit while I watch the television shows that no one else cries at, or I go online and look at photos of unlikely animal friendships, spending hours cooing at really aggressive-looking German Shepherds who are best friends with baby ducklings. Number 1 days are THE BEST. And I advocate that everyone has them once in a while.

I need my Number 1 Days, but for years I refused myself them. This was for a variety of reasons, but mostly because that's when I'd realise I was lonely, or I was scared, or the dark thoughts would come. It was on those quieter days that I thought about wanting a partner and realised I didn't think I could trust anybody because the break-up with my ex-fiancé had hurt me so badly. It was also on those days that I reflected on my bad decisions, and the times I snapped at people when I shouldn't have. In my twenties all that stuff used to catch up with me on my Number 1 Days. But now, because I am allowing myself down time, I'm less stressed, less rushed, less angry and I'm able to have a healthy relationship, to be kind to people. I don't totally lose my head if I can't find my Uber, I don't bark at the car service operator on my phone. I don't think the sky is falling if I misplace my phone. The smallest inconveniences don't send me into a spin anymore. Being a nicer person is easier when you allow yourself to embrace all your foibles and accept you sometimes need a break; you need time to recover and rest. When you stop pretending you're superhuman you're able to be a happier and healthier version of yourself. This acknowledgement, and my numbering of days, has played a huge part in my ability to balance my moods, my depression and my down times. When you pare back, you're not missing anything, you're just giving yourself the space and time to be a better you.

## Giving up guilt

Often my depression has been linked to my struggle with guilt. During my first meeting with my therapists, the Speakmans, before I went into the jungle, they were convinced I was a devout Catholic because the guilt I held about everything was so pronounced and problematic. I am working on it though. I think I'm incredibly hard on myself because for so long I did things I'm not proud of. I'm constantly playing catch-up, making my way up that sliding scale of being a good person. For years, I was late, and rude, and angry, and defensive, and made mistakes and hurt people. Probably some of you will be able to relate to this. When you're in your twenties, you're working out who you are. Some of you may still be in your twenties, and may not realise it, but in that decade, you can be a bit of an arsehole. Let's face it, I totally was, and my arsehole-ness was on a bigger scale because I had a bunch of people watching.

Now I'm thirty-three, I feel like I have to be the very best person I can, because for years I wasn't. I really wasn't. It's not painful to admit that anymore. I love this path I'm on now, and the patience and kindness I'm developing. I never had these things before. In my twenties I was incredibly self-absorbed and driven, to my detriment; I wasn't thoughtful, but I didn't think you needed to be thoughtful to be successful. Now, I do feel guilt probably a bit more than I should because of who I used to be, and because I'm still working on myself. I know there's a fair few people out there who don't see me as that loud, drunk girl on *Geordie Shore* anymore, or who only found me in the last few years on social media, or only started noticing me when I was on *MasterChef*, but I remember who I was. I remember the things I said and I remember the people I hurt. And I remember the things other people said to me, and what other people called me. Letting go of that isn't easy; it's an ongoing project.

I'd love to think when I'm seventy-five years old I'll be sitting on a porch swing somewhere, all wrinkly and happy, with a cute little sausage dog on my knee, and feeling carefree because by then I'll have lived forty or fifty years being a really epic, friendly, positive person . . . but there's a part of me that has to accept I'll have to live with what I did forever. And I'm okay with that.

If you're reading this and struggling with guilt over something you did in the past, or something you said, I'm with you, and I feel you. The truth is no one can just wipe the slate clean, but you can learn from your mistakes. You might not be able to forget what you did, and forgive what you may have done, but you can reclaim your power and decide to change, and from this day forward work harder to be thoughtful and considerate. Make your next day better.

## Exercising to exhaustion

Over the years, my relationship with exercise has completely evolved from something unhealthy – or something that I felt guilt over, as you can imagine from reading the previous section, if I didn't do enough – into a tool that helps my mental health. For years, I weaponised the concept of exercise and fitness, as I touched on in Chapter 2, using it as a punishment if I felt I'd overeaten, or as a punishment because I hated the way I looked. It was a form of self-harm. Don't get me wrong, I was incredibly strong and fit – I never exercised to the detriment of my health – but I didn't have healthy goals. I wasn't doing it because I wanted to wake up in the morning before my alarm clock feeling ready for the day, or because I was running a marathon for charity, or because I wanted to be the best, most energetic version of myself to be able to do everything I needed to do. I wasn't exercising for the many, many reasons you should. I was *not* working out so I could live longer, feel happier, be stronger. I was working out because I was in pursuit of an unachievable aesthetic, a visual idea of perfection, which I'd been led to believe would make me happy. And it ruled my life. And the irony of it is, it actually led me to be really, really unhappy.

Today, I can best describe my body type as *definitely likes to work out but never says no to a cookie*. It's just who I am. So now I train because I like the way it makes me feel. This is a weird example maybe, but recently I came home and there were four huge parcels left outside the house. I'm not talking just too big to fit through the letterbox, I'm talking nearly too big to get through my door. There were stools for the kitchen, and five packs of hangers, and I was so chuffed that I was fit and strong enough to get them in the house. I'm lucky enough to be well and able to do these kind of things, and as long as I am, I want to train hard to be as self-sufficient as I can be.

Today, I train so I'm capable and confident, so if I'm ever in a difficult situation, I feel mentally and physically prepared to handle it. I truly believe in a healthy body, healthy mind. There is such a link. I love any sort of physical exercise for what it does to my mood. I'm going away with my family for a weekend in the countryside soon, and my mam and sister love to take long walks in the fells, like a right pair of ramblers. I can't wait to pack a pair of boots so I can join them, get out into the fresh air, feel the rain on my face and keep walking for miles. I also love swimming, I like Pilates, a bit of yoga, I love chucking a few weights around. There's nothing I won't give a go and there's something very satisfying about getting your heart rate up and feeling – and proving – that you're strong. If any of you are reading this feeling lazy or lethargic, and you're looking for someone to motivate you, shouting at you to get out of bed and start working out, you've come to the wrong place. Sometimes I have days where I cannot be arsed. I totally believe in feeling your feels and listening to your body, and sometimes your body is just not meant to be pushed on a certain day, for a certain reason. I remember training once with my personal trainer, a guy who has been a constant source of kindness and positivity to me over the last decade. It was my second workout of the week and I'd lost my handbag somewhere because I was so stressed out, and he just said to me, 'It's not your day. Sometimes the best workout you can do is no workout. Be honest with yourself.'

But – but! – if you know you're in a couch potato state and you're just being a lazybones, do something chill and easy. Here's an example: when I can't be bothered to do anything really intense but I know I should move my body, I do something that doesn't feel like exercise. Recently, I got home from a longish day out working, and I unpacked loads of boxes I'd been putting off since I moved house, and then went upstairs and started working on my walk-in wardrobe. Use your home as a gym. You can put a wash on, empty the dishwasher – it's all physical. The job of a woman, the job of a mother, is hard. Never underestimate what you achieve and how much you move even when you're not actively thinking that you're exercising. Being active doesn't have to be a structured Pilates class or a PT session, it can be anything. Don't be so hard on yourself, do things that don't feel like it. In the summer, a swim is great – I love it. Whatever you can do that doesn't feel like a chore will really help you stay motivated to move. I always say, 'It doesn't have to feel like hell to be healthy.' And everyone can find that one thing that is really good for them that doesn't feel painful. If you hate something, you won't do it. If you hate Pilates or hate riding your bike, you won't do it, so stop trying to force it. Do a Zumba class. Try pole dancing. I go to puppy yoga sometimes, and I'll be totally honest with you and say not a lot of yoga gets done – I spend most of my time running around the room after the puppies – but it's still movement. If you're chasing puppies, you're burning calories, and that is a rule I live by!

Sometimes your body doesn't need to exercise; it needs a day off. Be in tune with your body. And if you miss a workout, don't feel bad. If you haven't moved your body at all today, don't fret. Do what you can tomorrow.

## My anxious mind

Exercise has helped me deal with another of my mental health concerns: anxiety. I've always been an intense overthinker, which I get from my dad. My inherited propensity to anxiety has really scared me at times because I've always been acutely aware my father chose to deal with it using alcohol. It's always in the back of my mind that I am my father's daughter, and my strategy to keep my anxiety at bay is to fill my life up to the max, to regiment it, to plan everything. I make notes and lists because if I do leave my mind to its own devices for too long, I'm scared of where it will go. I'm a Type A person. To explain, that means I have the Type A personality traits of being controlling, competitive and ambitious; as opposed to Type B people who are more flexible, less stressed and usually better at relaxing.

I am someone who likes to have things planned with military precision. I like to know where I'm going, what I'm wearing. I like to be on time, to know what's next, to have a clear plan. Being a control freak is my overthinking mind's coping mechanism; alcohol was my father's.

My life coach has talked to me about my anxiety loads, and told me that in order for people to get to the top of their game, pretty much, they have to be Type A. This sounds almost like a plus, but there are downsides. I'm aware that my desire to be in control all of the time can have negative ramifications, but the alternative isn't worth entertaining. The alternative is the person you saw on *Geordie Shore*, or the person you saw on a PR conveyor belt straight from the jungle, who went out every night, surrounded herself with people she couldn't trust and got drunk to calm the roaring feeling of stress and powerlessness that was forming in her mind. When I feel like things are going too fast and I'm losing control, I blow caution to the wind and just give in, go with it. I have to have lists, and I have to know what time I'm being picked up, and I have to know if the photoshoot is happening or not. Otherwise, it all gets too much.

Do you know how much I wish I was one of these super chilled people who just roll with the punches? Oh my god, how dreamy would that be? To be THAT girl! The relaxed girl, the flighty girl, the cool girl, the Type B girl perhaps. But sadly, I am the overscheduled, hypersensitive, sweaty girl. If I'm meeting my friends and my train's late, I over-apologise and stress and explain myself, and they're just like 'Yeah, no worries man, water off a duck's back.' I just wish I could be like that. The back of my knees sweat just at the thought of being late for something. It's frustrating that this is who I am sometimes, but relinquishing that control means giving up a certain degree of my sanity, and I've been there and done that, and if being this super-neurotic, high-performing overthinker is what I have to be to not descend into my darkness, then I'll put up with it.

This is a good time to mention that, in the history of the world, no one who has been told to calm down actually calms down. If anyone is reading this thinking *Vicky, you need to chill out*, I say: do you think I haven't tried?! Over the years I've had plenty of people who've encouraged me to take a slightly lighter approach to life, or relax, and it's hard. My mam now understands completely who I am after years of trying to work it out, and there are elements of her that are like this as well.

She says my problem is that I'm clever like my dad. My mam is very intelligent – she does herself a disservice when she says she's not – but she's not neurotic, so she doesn't overthink everything. People like me and my dad can turn a couple of hours of downtime into a dark place where you've taken yourself on an incredibly upsetting and toxic downward spiral. My mam encourages me to do things she loves that help her, like meditation and yoga. And I do love those things. I go to yoga, I go to Pilates, I meditate, I read, I've even got fucking apps that have rain sounds on my phone, for god's sake. You name it, I've got it – but I'm still this intense, excited, neurotic person, and I know I must drive her and everyone around me insane sometimes. My sister sometimes shouts at me, 'Will you just fucking sit down?' but I can't help myself. My nervousness, my anxiety, my constant need to be in control ... it manifests itself in different ways and I'm at the mercy of it a lot of the time. Which sounds pretty dismal when you say it like that, but I function this way and I have made my hyperactive brain and nervous disposition work for me.

I've harnessed the energy. I have a weekly to-do list that I will write out on a Sunday, and it will include everything from what I'm going to eat, to if and how I'm going to work out, to what I'm going to post on Instagram, to going to the post office, to sorting my clothes to do a white wash. It's in my notes on my phone and I couldn't function without it. Then I have a daily to-do list, too. It's less, *get to Manchester, do that photoshoot* and more *throw out the old flowers, empty the dishwasher.* Less glam, more mundane but equally important to making my mind a calm and happy little place. It helps because if I let the washing build up, or the house is in desperate need of a vacuum, it adds to the feeling of chaos and being out of control in my mind. These two to-do lists help me keep on track in tandem. The weekly one is to make sure I'm achieving what I need to achieve, forging forward to reach my long-term goals, *and* I keep my daily one on track so my life is in order and I know the weekly aims are possible. I mean, I even add things to my to-do list after I've done them to give myself extra credit. Like when I've just done something absent-mindedly, I'll go back and add it. Yep, I am very much that sad cow!

My advice to you – don't be ashamed to live by lists. They help! I live by lists to the point I'm turning into Monica from *Friends*. Remember in that episode after Phoebe's wedding, when she's ticking off everything, and Chandler says to her, 'Is there any room on that thing for us to have sex?' That's me. I'll properly plan if Ercan and I are going to have sex – I have to! – so I can make sure I've had a bath, I've shaved, I haven't just had a spray tan, and we have enough time. I mean the poor fella, he puts up with it, but I'm sure he wishes I was a bit more footloose and fancy free and chucked him a quickie on a Sunday night once in a while. But no. If it's not on the list, it's not happening, sunshine.

The best bit of advice I got about handling my anxiety, which I hope will help you, is this: a good amount of planning, nerves and excitement are fine, and prove you're invested in what you're doing. It's when those feelings start to turn into anxiety and stress that you know you are trying to control the uncontrollable.

A good example of this was the COVID-19 pandemic we've all gone through. Even the most easygoing person experienced feelings of hopelessness, and even though everyone was going through it together, it didn't make it any easier. I realised very quickly, with the help of my life coach I'd like to add, that I was sitting worrying and winding myself up about stuff so far out of the perimeters of my control. I was worried about people dying, when the pandemic would be finished, when I could go back to work, when I could see my family, when could normal life resume, when I could hug my friends again, when I could go on holiday . . . all things that were outside of my control. There is no way one tiny person can control all this. All you're doing when you're expelling so much of your energy on that is exhausting yourself, and most probably worrying yourself into a very dark and sad little hole.

Instead, I've learnt to focus my energy on the stuff I can control, things that bring me comfort and purpose, and make me feel proactive. I focus on what will help me feel calm. So instead of worrying whether I would ever go back to work or see my mam again, I focused on getting up in the morning, making sure I exercised, and figured out how I could work from home – so I wasn't just sitting around with my finger up my arse. I made sure that mentally and physically I was in the best possible place to deal with the upset and uncertainty that was happening all around me. I started my podcast. I worked on social campaigns, and tried hard to use my Instagram as a platform to spread kindness and positivity. Instead of worrying so much about myself, I started thinking about how I could help others. I started an isolation care package project, which allowed me to help feed vulnerable and elderly people. Every week, I'd get in touch with big brands and ask them to make donations. On a Thursday, I'd get together with mates in a friend's warehouse and we'd pack boxes of food and get them out to members of the community who needed them. It was so rewarding to give back to the community, but it also helped me get through the pandemic. Once I started to take control of the things I *could* control, I felt better, and it gave me focus and stopped me feeling so powerless, lost and anxious.

That was the best piece of advice that I ever got: there are uncontrollables in your life and you're just going to have to accept that. Try to pop those things to the back of your mind, focus on the things you can control and do the best with what you have – and honestly, that's what got me through the various lockdowns and difficult days, and it's what I'll take forward with me throughout my life.

## Sleepy time

A symptom of my anxiety has always been my difficulty in sleeping. For a long time, as you may deduce from the long list of issues above, I was what you'd describe as an insomniac. In any given week, I'd have three nights where sleep completely evaded me and I'd have to go to work exhausted. I've always had an overactive imagination and switching off my brain has never been easy, but the more my life was pushed into the public eye, and the more pressure I felt on me, the worse it became. This issue really came to a head post-jungle. I was constantly under a microscope and I struggled to deal with that, and it was such a shock after having the best sleep of my life when I was actually in *I'm a Celebrity*. That's why I've got the app I mentioned before – you know, the one with the rain sounds? Well, it also has campfire sounds. Stroke of genius! Honestly, it was weird, but despite the circumstances, the fact that you know there are millions of people watching and you can hear cameras whirring constantly, I managed to sleep so soundly in the jungle. The crew get you up really early – as soon the light comes up, at 5 a.m., 6 a.m. – in order to start recording the show, which I'm sure for some of you guys with kids might seem like a blissful lie-in but for little old me, single and childless, it felt like the middle of the night. And if you've done a trial or a dingo dollar challenge throughout the day, chances are you've walked a lot. In order to make the often impressive looking and huge trials they needed a lot of space, so the locations could be quite far away from the actual camp, and the only way through the jungle was by foot. When you've not got a lot of calories in your tummy that can seriously wipe you out. Also, the heat was exhausting; one day I did a trial in fifty degrees, and for a pasty little Geordie like me that was gruelling. I still believe though that the reason I was able to switch off and sleep so well in the jungle was because we weren't allowed our phones or any other technology. Without the lure of technology, you'd be amazed at how quickly you can relax and fall asleep – although saying that, I bet most of you are already painfully aware of the crippling obsessive hold our emails, Instagram accounts and WhatsApp messages have on us. I think we can all be a little guilty sometimes of having an unhealthy relationship with our phones – I know mine is practically a permanent fixture in my hand and when it is I very rarely stop working. I answer emails, check my WhatsApp, double check my diary, scan my social media posts, all of which has added massively to my anxiety and stress levels. And without all of that technological distraction, I had no choice but to sleep at night. It was the best consistent sleep I've ever had, and I've always chased that feeling since.

For someone like me who is so overwhelmingly fearful of missing anything – who has cripplingly bad FOMO, coupled with the fear of being late – sleep started to elude me post-jungle. If I was due to be a guest on a breakfast television show, which I had to be up at 4 a.m. for, and I've come in from a night-time recording at 11 p.m. the night before, the pressure of knowing I only had five hours to get my head down, get some sleep, would be too much to allow me to drift off, and I'd sit in bed watching the minutes tick by.

We've all had those conversations with ourselves, haven't we? There are so many memes about it. When you tell yourself, *right, if I fall asleep within a minute, I can still get five hours sleep* ... then an hour goes by ... *right, if I fall asleep right now, I can still get four hours sleep.* On these nights, I used to just give up, and accept I'd be tired, knowing that if I slept a little bit, it would probably be worse for me and I'd wake up groggy. I gave up fighting with myself, lying in bed with my mind taking me on a trip down memory lane, regurgitating all my mistakes. It's my brain's party trick when it really wants to punish me, when my body is trying to go to sleep and my mind really doesn't want it to. My brain says, 'So you think you're in charge, eh? Aww, you silly little fool. I AM IN

CHARGE. So here is a collection of some of your most embarrassing moments from over the last ten years. Would you like to start with the time you got engaged on the telly, or perhaps the time you were drunk and slurring your words when thousands of people were watching you?'

I gave up trying to make my mind do what it clearly didn't want to do because I was so terrified of where it would take me. Consequently my insomnia just spiralled. Looking back, I wasn't the best version of myself at that time. I was just surviving. I had to take loads of Beroccas, Pro-Plus and all sorts of stuff. I used to have a Red Bull every day before 10 a.m.! The thought of that now makes me physically sick, but back then it was the norm. I really abused fat-burners too, which was less about my weight – although of course, I was still desperate to look a certain way at this point too – but more to keep me awake. It was a really toxic time, but I was so fried and had nothing left in me.

Today is better on the sleep front. I compare that Vicky to the Vicky I am now, when I'm probably the healthiest I've ever been. My mind still pesters me when I'm trying to relax and sometimes it'll still keep me up at night, but I'm much kinder to myself than I was. I'm able to have good relationships with the people around me – whether it be working relationships or personal ones, I treat people with kindness and respect (including myself), I'm not so stressed, I'm still high performing but not tortured – and that all helps me sleep better.

I give credit for my improved sleep to my change in attitude more than any sleep app or lavender spray. I have always found it hardest to sleep when I knew I hadn't been a nice person that day. If I had treated someone badly, or said something I shouldn't, or argued with someone, or made my agent's life difficult, or been rude to a makeup artist, I wouldn't sleep. I wasn't doing those things because I was a bad person, I was doing them because I was exhausted. And then of course, after I'd behaved terribly, I wouldn't sleep again – guilt, shame and frustration kept me awake. I'm sure you can see the vicious cycle emerging. The minute I did these horrible things, I knew I'd be up all night thinking about them, torturing myself. It was a constant cycle of being snappy, feeling overworked, being rude, feeling exhausted, and before you know it, lying awake all night again.

I've made a conscious effort now, not only because I want to be nicer and I don't want to be known as a knob, but ultimately, because it'll cause me to lie awake overanalysing my behaviour at night. That phrase 'I don't know how he can sleep at night' – I think about that a lot. Typical of an overthinker, I know. But unless you're a psychopath, I do not know how people can act poorly, treat people badly and generally just be an arse-hole and then still sleep at night. One of my exes was a pretty cruel man. He wasn't physically abusive but he lacked empathy – and looking back now, I realise it was incredible I ever thought we had a future – because I have all of the feelings and he had none. He would say the meanest things to me in bed, then just turn over, and within minutes, he would be lying back with his hands behind his head in a deep sleep, snoring, the epitome of carefree slumber. I'd take myself off to the sofa and lie there wide awake thinking that was my future: a man who didn't care and could sleep soundly during my emotional torture. I'd lie there in the dark, crying, and think *how can you sleep at night?*

The fact is, however soundly he slept, I do not want to be like him and I do want to sleep, so I've had an attitude adjustment. This change has affected a lot of things, my improved sleep being one of them, but also how I am on social media. Now if someone comes for me, and trolls me, I can let it go. In the past, I wouldn't have been able to. There was this one interaction that stands out. I'd posted a picture of me in a fur gilet. Of course, it wasn't real fur. I mean, what kind of nutcase would I have to be to wear a real fur gilet? Anyway, this woman came for me. 'You're a fucking disgrace. How dare you kill an animal to wear it around your neck!' I actually replied and wrote, 'You fucking idiot. Do you actually think I'd kill an animal just to wear it? Before you come for me, do your fucking research, and don't ever come at me like that again or I will end up wearing you round my neck.' I literally wrote that! Someone sent it to me recently and I read it and thought, *who is that person?* No wonder I didn't sleep! If I spoke to anyone like that now I wouldn't be able to sleep for a month.

I've read everything the experts tell you about how to cure insomnia – have your bedroom at a certain temperature, wear a cotton nightie, cover yourself in oil, have a warm bath, don't eat too much before bedtime – and I've been given so much advice by therapists, and life coaches and personal trainers, and I've bought fancy sleep sprays and eye masks, and downloaded all the relaxation apps ever made. I even once bought a special box for my phone. A box that I had to put my phone in and move away from my bed, so that when sleep eluded me, I couldn't just roll over and stare at the bright screen of my phone, which makes insomnia worse. I put the phone in the box, locked it, and took it to the other side of the room. And of course, it didn't deter me. I just got up and got it! I don't know what kind of person that would work for, but it was a waste of money for me.

The one thing that did work for me was being physical, if you can – whether that's tidying the house, walking the dog, doing a pole dancing class or running 10k. I dare you to try it and not get a better night's sleep.

And being kind, to others and to myself, of course. If you put your best foot forward, if you're nice to people, if you strive to make others feel comfortable, if you remember your pleases and thank yous, if you are respectful, if you're thoughtful, if you're courteous – all these things help you sleep better. You'll be able to get into bed at night and relax. You can get under the duvet with less to worry about.

Every so often, yes, the fact I had sex on television will pop up, and stop me from sleeping; or the time I was rude to a taxi driver in 2008, or the argument with my mam from 2005 . . . I can't guarantee you will never have flashbacks, but if you're always striving to be better, when you close your eyes there are fewer demons to keep you awake.

## Sense and sensitivity

A very real side effect of being tired all the time is that my already sensitive nature gets even more pronounced. I used to hate being sensitive, and I'd try to hide from my vulnerabilities. Someone could tell me a sad story about their life, and they wouldn't cry but I'd be sobbing, in floods of tears, worried they'd think I was belittling their pain, and unable to pull myself together. *What right have you got – when they're fine – to sob like this*, I'd admonish myself. But now I embrace it and accept it's so much of who I am, and how I'm made, and it's not all bad. I'm the kind of person that if you walk into a room, and you're sad, I'll feel it and be sad too. If you come home and you've had a bad day, I'll know it. If you're sad, anxious or low, I'll know it. I'll absorb it. I match energies. Even if I've had a shit day, if I meet someone who is buzzing with positivity, I'll start to buzz too. It helps me relate to others in a sympathetic way. I can understand what they're feeling, and that allows me to get closer to people, which in turn has helped me to forge better, deeper friendships.

It was my life coach who helped me understand how and why I am like I am – I cried on the phone within the first five minutes of speaking to him during our first session, so he had me pegged as an HSP (a Highly Sensitive Person) straight away. He told me 5–10 per cent of the world fall into this HSP category and it's explained loads. It still does! It explains why I possibly struggle to sleep, why I cry at the drop of a hat, why things hurt me that don't hurt others. I used to run from it because I hated that side of me, now I've learned to embrace it and look at all the good things it gives me. Being an empath, as so many of you are reading this now, I'm sure, can make your life a bit harder, but it can make the lives of people around you, who you love and care about, a little bit nicer – and that is the biggest plus!

It means your friends don't have to go through anything alone. Your family knows you always feel how they're feeling and they can tell you anything without fear of judgement. People know you love them, under-stand them and will be right there with them. But it's draining. It's exhausting. I have enough emotions of my own; I'm a real rollercoaster over here without getting everyone else to jump on the ride with me. If Laura has an argument with her boss, or my mam has a fallout with my dad, I feel it. If you're similar, be aware of the pluses and minuses of this personality type. But if you're this kind of person, you do have to look after your mental health. I don't mind being like this if it means my friends get a good friend, and my mum gets a good daughter, but it's why I've had to be more specific and choosier about who I spend my time with – something we could all do more of, to be fair. If people around you are constantly being angry, disrespectful, rude or hostile, you will soak that in – you won't be able to help yourself. You're porous! It's quite easy for me, if I'm around those kinds of people, to start displaying those traits too, so I've learnt to distance myself from them in order to protect my peace. It's something I've learnt the hard way, through friendships with people who were always looking for a drama, or constantly moaning that the world was against them. I noticed I was becoming like them, after being with them for just a couple of hours, and it wasn't good.

I've realised, because of who I am and how my brain is wired, I have to choose the people in my life very carefully. Being wise about my relationships has been the biggest safeguard for my mental health. I've learnt what my triggers are, and can spot a mile off if I'm working my way up to something. Before, in my twenties, I just used to press ahead and then let it blow up in my face, making a massive mess that would cover everyone around me in chunks of crazy Vicky.

## Listen out for your warning bells

I've spotted my patterns now. I can see the early warning signs of when my mental health is starting to deteriorate. First, I'll start to make small mistakes, like forgetting my phone, misplacing my keys. I know I'm overworked, trying to do too much, or I'm overtired and my brain is full of too many things. And I can recognise that now, and allow myself to take a break. It sounds silly and simple, but it's really helped me: just taking a break when I start noticing little things sliding.

If I don't take a break, the next stage is to blame other people. When I'm a bit more level, I can say 'Oh, I couldn't find my Uber, and it's fine' – it happens, it's part of life, sometimes cars don't find you and some- times you're standing in the wrong place. Whatever. But if I'm tired it changes, and I'm easily triggered and usually looking for someone to blame – it would be more like 'my Uber driver is an idiot.' That is what I go to. And it's unhealthy, and it's incorrect and you're on a road to nowhere. Another example would be if I'm late and I miss a train because I've done a radio interview. I'll moan and say it's everyone else's fault for overbooking me. It's never my fault for mismanaging my time. We all do that. We all look for people to blame when things are going wrong, or getting out of control, or when we're stressed or tired. Maybe it feels easier in the short term, but it doesn't work. What we need to do in the long term is pull ourselves back from that. Blaming everyone else for your shit is not a nice trait.

If I don't take a break after the blame stage, the next step is usually intense anger. I'm aware this makes me sound like the Hulk – and for anyone that has watched me on *Geordie Shore*, you will know that Bruce Banner's alter ego and I actually have far more in common than is ideal. I've spent years cultivating a life that doesn't make me angry; I've avoided situations that could potentially be triggering and make me angry and cut out people who frustrate me. For example, I'm owning now that I'm not a nightclub person after years of trying to be. I like to talk to people and hear their answers. My ideal night would be a bunch of brilliant, clever, witty people sitting around a table sharing delicious food, drinking great wine, sharing stories, chatting about our childhoods and discussing our hopes and dreams for the future. That is what I like and that is who I am. I hate being in a nightclub – I hate the smells, I hate being pushed, I hate having to queue for the toilets,

I hate not being able to hear anybody. These things make me agitated, so I've admitted that and I avoid them. I have worked hard and made conscious changes to my life to ensure I'm not in situations that make me frustrated if I can help it. Which is why I know, if I feel anger rising in me over silly little things, it's time to have a Number 1 Day. A day when I don't go on social media, and I just watch the shows that make me laugh and cry, eat the stuff I know I shouldn't all the time – party rings, pizza and pasta, the three Ps.

Being able to recognise your triggers, the signs you've had enough, is crucial. And when you do see the signs, don't be harsh on yourself. Don't criticise your needs and call yourself a weak bitch. You are powerful beyond measure, and even queens need help adjusting their crowns somedays. Allow yourself a bad day, a moment of weakness, and then take a breath and start again tomorrow. Progress, not perfection, ladies.

# The Secret To... boosting your mental health

* Do things that make you feel okay. Look after yourself. Take a break and unwind. Remember – cherish those Number 1 Days when you can turn everything off, or turn it down, and give yourself a break.

* Do a face mask and chill out while you watch your favourite childhood movie, preferably with snacks. Little luxuries like this will give you the boosts you need to get you through the week.

* Jump in a bubble bath with a good book or glossy magazine – the escapism offered when you read other people's stories, fiction or non-fiction, can help you forget about your current woes, give you some perspective, or offer a new way of looking at a problem.

* Do a yoga class. The benefits of getting some endorphins flowing through your body, then letting the endorphins rush your brain, are not to be underestimated. Indeed, any physical exercise that you enjoy will help you feel better about your body, will give your brain a dash of positivity and uplift your whole day.

* Meditate (if you can. No shade if you can't because I am STILL working on that one!). It is known to lower those stress-inducing cortisol levels.

* Pour yourself a glass of wine, turn up some music and have a one-person disco in your front room. Dancing is a known mood lifter, and listening to music that fills you with nostalgia for happy times is a surefire way to increase glee.

* Art and craft your way to the zone-out zone: paint, write, knit, crochet, draw, take photos, press flowers (this is a type of meditation for people who can't meditate, these hobbies can help you to zone out from the real world for a bit).

* Get outside and connect with nature. Go for a walk in the park, along a river, at the seaside. Take in sunshine and fresh air. The vitamin D you get outside will help you sleep better, and all your cobwebs will blow away.

* Lastly, and this is the most important one … DO WHATEVER THE FUCK YOU WANT AS LONG AS IT BRINGS YOU PEACE.

## PREPARE YOUR PURPOSE

Use the section below over the next two weeks, and number each day as you go. Remember: super busy days are a 4, kind of busy days are a 3, normal days are a 2 and chilled days are a 1. Recognise when you need a break, or when you've felt that you could do more as you work your way through your week. Numbering your days and making sure you are looking after yourself can boost happiness – professionally and personally. I used to think that in order to be successful and to be a high performer, all my days had to be jam-packed from morning till night, that you should never need or want a day off. But you can't do that. You'll burn out. You won't be the best version of yourself. Every task you give yourself to will be getting a half version of you, a tortured version of you, an exhausted version of you! After your week making notes below, go through your diary or calendar and mark each with a number. If you need more Number 1 Days on the sofa with a Netflix marathon and a bowl of Cadbury's Mini Eggs, write them in and don't allow other people to take that time from you. If you don't have enough Number 4 Days going on to keep you motivated and focused, book purposeful, rewarding things in. Push yourself. Scan your diary on a weekly or monthly basis and look for balance.

| Date | Number (1–4) | Notes |
|------|--------------|-------|
|      |              |       |
|      |              |       |
|      |              |       |
|      |              |       |
|      |              |       |
|      |              |       |
|      |              |       |

| Date | Number (1–4) | Notes |
|------|--------------|-------|
|      |              |       |
|      |              |       |
|      |              |       |
|      |              |       |
|      |              |       |
|      |              |       |
|      |              |       |

# 7

# Skills for social media

*Comparison is the thief of joy.*

Believe it or not, considering how obsessed with it I am now, I really was reluctant to get involved with social media. I had to be forced to join Twitter by MTV, back in my *Geordie Shore* days. I thought, *who's going to want to listen to what I've got to say? No one will follow me.* I suppose I got that a bit wrong. Instagram took me even longer to get my head round; I didn't get it. It was just pictures, and again I thought, *who is going to want to see loads of pictures of me?* Wrong again Vicky, you numpty. Today I have conflicted feelings about social media. There are clear pluses and minuses to our obsession with what goes on online. But I am grateful for loads of things, so let's count the blessings first.

Let's call a spade a spade. It brings me loads of work and it's how I generate a lot of my income, and

I know many of you with small businesses, online companies, mummy blogs, travel blogs or anything in between will feel the same. It's a great platform for us all to show off our creativity, to share our business and what we're doing professionally. If someone is an artist, or a photographer, or a writer, it's great for them to use it as a resource to share their portfolios and ideas.

Social media is great because it is ours to control, which allows us to be powerful. To take ownership of our content. When I do an interview, my words go into the ears of a journalist and then get interpreted by them. So much gets lost in translation, whether it's intentional or unintentional – the jury is still out on that one for me – but it ends up not being verbatim, and suddenly my thoughts, feelings and messaging are muddled. My social media is mine, and I'm able to express myself well on there. I love that I'm able to think things and they go straight from my brain to my fingertips to the screen into the hearts and heads of Sarah from Salisbury, Claire from Cork or Anna from Aberdeen. And when they read my posts, they know how I feel and I know they have been there, too. When I write about these personal things, I know a lot of you will going through them as well. I know some ladies will also be on their period, or be hungover, or be having a bad day. I know that when I share, and people like or comment or even just look at my posts, we all feel a little less alone. It's my way of connecting with people all over the country, and all over the world.

And we can't forget there are so many of us running a hundred miles a day, who just don't have the time to connect with their friends and family in person, or to be there for every event, every important moment, or have an in-depth, in-person catch-up. Social media is such a good way to touch base and stay in contact. I live down south and my family and oldest friends are all up north. I can't just pop to the pub, sit down with them, chat about their day and slag off their boss – that little round trip takes me around eight hours. But because I see their photos and news on social media, I still feel involved, close to them and up to date on all the gossip. I love that I don't have to miss anything with my friends' kids, too. I know if Jacob has won a star pupil award, or if Mavie has learnt a new word or Harley has turned six months or if Franky got a hair-cut. When there's a great distance between you and the people you love, that connection is priceless. I do live a long way away, and it helps with homesickness. It's built a bridge for me living so far away from those in my life who I love the most – and it has allowed me to reconnect with people I'd lost touch with. One of my best friends from university, Zoe, for example – we'd left uni and lost contact as we moved back to our respective hometowns, but we found each other again on social media, and she's having a baby and married to the guy she was dating at uni who I loved, which was wonderful to find out. Now we speak every week, she is one of my favourite people in the world and my girls all absolutely adore her. I'm able to see all these lives, even when I'm not in Newcastle or Bolton or Bangkok or Sydney – wherever my friends are – and it's lush. To be able to jump into all these lives around the world at a touch of a button is a terrific feat of technology, and that's why I can't totally knock it – for those three reasons: opportunity, power and connection.

## Anti-social media

But of course, there are downsides.

I don't think it matters if you have five followers or five million followers, social media has created a culture where people think it's acceptable to write things from behind a screen that, in the real world, they'd get punched in the face for saying. I offer zero apologies for saying this. Violence is bad, I know, but social media has created this really nasty, unwisely bold movement where people think they can say whatever they want, declaring it free speech or that they're just being honest, and it upsets me deeply. No, you are not expressing your freedom of speech or honesty, you're being rude. You are being a bully. And if you wouldn't say these things to someone's face you have zero right to say them across social media. I can't impress enough on anyone reading this that we all have to remember that there are others sitting and reading and ingesting the callous, vile sentiments that some people – hopefully not you, or anyone you know – are spewing from their phone or laptop. It's beyond me. Being active on social media comes with a moral responsibility. It is an abuse of the freedom those platforms give you to write or say harmful things about others.

I'm not an actress. I'm not in a big soap where everyone sees me as this character I'm portraying on telly, three nights a week, for ten years. No, I'm famous for being me. For being myself. So, I can't distance myself from the things you think I am, from the information and insights you've garnered from me over the years, whether it's following me on social media, watching my shows, reading my books, working out to my exercise DVDs – whatever. You are actually attacking who I am, and there's no way in a million years that I'm not going to take that personally. How do people not make that connection? Whether you're speaking to someone across a crowded table or across a computer screen, your words will get into the ears of that person, and then into their heart. It affects their mood and how they see themselves.

Tragically, over the past decade, we have seen the damaging effect social media has had on so many people. We've lost enough beautiful, bright young people because of the vile insults and abuse they've received online – and yet, here we are, and I *still* have to beg at least once a month for people to be more courteous and decent on social media. It beggars belief! I'm bored of asking people to be kinder, to understand the power of their words, to think about the person who will receive their comment before they type. I suffer just a fraction of what some people get, but I know I will never stop demanding that people be kinder across social media. We have no idea what is going on in other people's lives. They could have lost their job, their home, or someone they love. And yet, some people still feel the need to spend their time spreading hate on the internet. Who does this? I imagine it's sad, lonely men who are living in their mother's box room, but it could be anyone. It could be that woman at the school gates who you think, *oh, Sandra, she's nice! Sweet kids, nice husband, great job, she's normal* – and then you find out she's sitting at her kitchen island late at night and sending horrible messages to someone from *TOWIE*. I like to think that's rare, though. Don't get me wrong, I've been caught out a few times with this train of thought. On occasion, curiosity has gotten the better of me and I've gone to look at the profile of whoever has written a rude or nasty comment to me on my page and it'll be a woman with 'live, laugh, love' in her bio, or 'my kids are my world', or 'I don't know what I'd do without my beautiful daughters' . . . and I think to myself, *I'm actually just someone's daughter too, Sandra.*

I used to believe that if I didn't take myself too seriously on social media, if I showed my good and bad sides, shared my highs and my lows, my glam days and my rough days, that people would relate to me and be kind. Most people who follow me are like that; they're kind, uplifting and positive people. But there are still others who just come to my page to be nasty, and they leave me at a loss. Nothing I do will ever get their respect or approval. There are people who will just hate me no matter what I do – whether it's sharing another photo of my period belly or my spotty face. And for a natural-born people pleaser like myself, who absolutely thrives on being liked, this is an incredibly difficult pill to swallow.

I will always encourage women to be honest and share real photos on social media, because only sharing filtered, perfect versions of yourself is unfair. It sets unrealistic expectations, and puts too much pressure on the person posting and the person consuming the post. We collectively cultivate this really unhealthy, toxic image of perfect being normal – which then of course leaves 'normal' looking undesirable. I don't think that has any positives. But when there are some people showing their best, edited, filtered lives online, and others like me doing the opposite – I show you wrinkles, I show you hangovers, I show you my sweaty, post-workout face – getting so much hate, you know it's nothing to do with content. All the blame goes to the trolls.

## Life isn't all peachy

Here is my explanation – one that I've unfortunately had to come to the hard way – about why even when you are honest and balanced on social media, you're still going to get trolled and hated. It's simple: not everyone is going to like you. As in real life, it's the same on social media. We are told this from when we're tiny, in the school playground, but it never gets any easier to accept. From childhood, humans are programmed to want to be liked. It's human nature to want to hear nice things said about you, to want to hear compliments. But what we have to understand is, the bigger your platform and the more accessible you are, the more you open yourself up to people who have no interest in being nice to you. Sometimes their specific reason for going on your page is because they *don't* like you and they don't want to understand you. It's been hard for me to accept over the years – the fact that there are people committed to misunderstanding me, to hating me and to criticising me. It doesn't matter how many charities I work with, how many reality shows I win, how many times I get my heart broken, I am always just a target. They will never feel sorry for me, or change how they feel about me. In their story, I am the villain.

My friend Lucy Spraggan told me a little story once, about peaches, and it's always stayed with me and provided me with solace when the trolls get me down. She said that you could be the best peach, the sweetest peach, the ripest peach on the tree; you could be fluffy, and plump, and juicy, and everyone will want to eat you because you are the best peach in the whole wide world. But then someone will come along who just doesn't like peaches. And there is nothing anyone can do about that! I've repeated that analogy countless times to people, and I have to remind myself of it all the time. Because you can be the nicest person, with the warmest disposition. You could be a hugely talented Oscar-winning actress, or an Olympic swimmer. You could do lots of things for charity and your community. You could be a good friend, partner or daughter. And you can try every day to uplift the people you interact with – be all the good things ... and someone will still come along who doesn't like peaches.

And your job, when this happens, is to remember you can't please all the people all the time. And it's not a reflection on you, how you present yourself or what you're doing. It usually says more about them, and their negative state of mind and nasty inner thoughts, than anything you've shared or said.

## Terrible trolls

I posted a tribute to Caroline Flack, who passed away in February 2020, on the one-year anniversary of her death. She was such a wonderful person, so full of life, vibrant and kind, and one of the first people to reach out to me when my ex-boyfriend did what he did. She was always at the end of the phone for me when I was struggling to cope. She still had so much to give, and her death rocked me to my core. So, on this tragic anniversary, I wrote this little tribute to honour her memory. I just tried to share how I felt. I said that without her in it, the world has just been a little bit quieter, a little less bright, and that she was missed – and someone slid into my DMs to tell me that I was fucking psychotic for grieving on Instagram, and that I didn't even fucking know her anyway, and that I was a fake bitch. They finished their rant by telling me if there was any justice in the world, I'd go the same way Caroline did. I still cry now thinking about what they wrote to me. I thought to myself, this woman has lost her life and all I'm doing is grieving in my own way, trying to raise a little bit of awareness for what she went through, and how she thought that was her only way out, and urging everyone to be a little bit better – nothing harmful. Yet here's someone wishing the same thing on me: death. And I remember ringing my sister in floods of tears because I just couldn't understand it.

Yes, over the years, I've had people attack the way I look. I had all the 'fat slag' comments you like when I was on *Geordie Shore*, and as I've got older I've had various things about how I look, and about the men I decide to go out with and how I deserve to be cheated on, and the 'here she goes again, on to the next, you'll be crying again any day now over him.' Some trolls are worse than others, and on the sliding scale of trolling there are certainly some comments I can deal with and some I can't. It goes from the cruel to the ridiculous. The other day, some woman told me that I had too many teeth in my mouth. Just to be clear, I have the same number of teeth I've always had and I've been assured by many dentists over the years that I have the correct amount. I'm not sure if people are in the habit of cramming more teeth into their mouth, but it sounds impossible and painful and certainly not something I'd be interested in. The comment was less about my gnashers anyway, it was more just another crazy way to try and pull apart my appearance and damage my confidence. Things like that I tend to be able to deal with, whether I laugh about it, just ignore it or choose to call the person out – give them their moment in the spotlight that they clearly so desperately crave. However, the comment I received off the back of my post about Caroline was really the worst. I was so heartbroken I kept the post up but deleted the conversation and blocked the person.

Please don't ever think that, just because someone has been in the industry for ten years or is always active on social media or is seemingly so well adjusted, that these hurtful and vile comments won't affect them. I'm yet to meet someone who can take constant criticism from strangers online on the chin. When I first spot a bad comment, my heart starts to beat fast and that fear takes over. It comes over me like a cold sweat. It's horrible to know there are people out there that think those things about you. But it's even worse because you're reading it while sitting on your sofa in your home and it almost feels like they're in your home with you, on your shoulder, in your space. It's so invasive because you can feel attacked in the one place you're supposed to feel the safest. And it's pretty hard to just let it wash over you in those circumstances. A lot of the time when it comes to online criticism I get these fellas – and you can tell it's a bloke by their display picture – and I'll be trying to write something nice, maybe something that encourages women to love the skin they're in, or wanting women to be able to order what they want in a restaurant and not have their self-worth so hinged on their weight – and out of the blue these blokes will write underneath my positive message, 'You got shagged on the telly.'

And in that moment a myriad of emotions and thoughts swirl through my mind. I'm angry, I'm sad, I'm embarrassed, I'm embarrassed for the fella who wrote it, I laugh because it's so long ago that I almost don't even see myself as that girl anymore and then I'm scared that if I've got a new follower, and they think I'm this really lovely, positive and kind person, they will see it and their opinion of me will change in an instant. But the overriding emotion I feel is frustration. I think, *how dare you, you tiny little man, be so intimidated by my personal growth and the woman I'm becoming that you're trying to drag me back to being that scared misguided little girl. Well, you won't! You won't scare me! You won't intimidate me! And you won't embarrass me! Not anymore.*

I've spent years beating myself up about the decisions I made when I was young and lost. I've bettered myself, I've built a better mindset, I'm happier and more confident (and a grown fucking woman, I might add), and I've built a place of positivity and kindness on social media. If that somehow offends you, if it holds a mirror up to your shortcomings, intimidates you, and makes you want to try and make me feel small, you can't. I've worked too hard to be this woman and no one is going to take that away from me.

## Keep calm and carry on – or delete and block?

I'm really lucky and generally, across the board, I get complimentary and kind things said to me on my social media accounts, and I hope you do too. But remember, when the downside emerges, you can handle it however you choose – there is no right or wrong way, or too harsh a reaction. Your account, your decision. No one should judge you on how you want to handle it. It's subjective. And your ability to cope with it could change, too. Some days, it'll be like water off a duck's back. On days when I've worked out, eaten well, and got a date night to look forward to – and I'm in that golden window when my hormones are normal and everything is just clicking – if someone writes something nasty about me I'll just think, *calm down, you're clearly having a bad day, I hope it gets better* and let it go. Because I'm content and they can't touch my peace. They can't bring me down.

But sometimes a nasty comment pops up, and we can't forget it, can we? Maybe you're having a crap day; you're missing your mam, or you had an argument with a friend, you're on your period or you're worried about your job, and when someone is unkind on social media it can send you over the edge. And when they hit you at the wrong time, you are allowed to deal with that however you wish. You reserve the right not to take it. I know that might not sound healthy, and it's probably not what a million other people would advise you to do, but it's your account and they're your feelings, so if you want to tell them not to hurt you, you can do so whichever way you see fit! Tell them to get off your page, tell them they're out of order, and if you want to block them and delete their comments that's okay too. If you want to screenshot what they wrote and share it on your page to humiliate them – that's your prerogative ... but please think very carefully before you do this. Remember these keyboard bullies are crying out for attention, they want to be noticed. They're not going to see it and think, *right, so-and-so has just highlighted my cruelty, I have seen the error of my ways, I realise now she is not a raving arsehole, it was in fact me who was acting like the aforementioned arsehole and now I'm going to endeavour to change and be better.* They're just not. They're going to complain, they're going to be even more bitter and twisted. 'Have you seen this fucking woman? Have you seen what she's done to me? She is a bitch, isn't she?' You feed the troll, you see, and just like gremlins after midnight, you should never feed the troll. You're validating them, unfortunately, and even though it may feel good in the heat of the moment, that feeling is fleeting. Whenever I do it, I'm always filled with remorse. I always end up thinking I should have done better, should have turned the other cheek rather than play their sad little game. So, honestly, do it if it will bring you some joy or peace but be careful, because if you're a nice person it will probably only end up making you feel worse. Take my word for it.

My relationship with social media, as you can tell, is still in its infancy. Although I'm thirty-three, and have had it since I was about twenty-five, it's still a short time to come to terms with it, with all the pros and cons. It's something I'm sure a lot of you still struggle with, too. So, my advice on this is to be taken with a pinch of salt as I am always, ALWAYS making mistakes online and getting myself into hot water. But the best advice I can give anyone is that the block button is there for a reason: use it as you see fit. No one, I repeat no one, has the right to make you feel bad on social media. If they are, block them, forget them, leave them to their misery and bitterness and enjoy your peace. Failing that, Scarlett Moffatt once told me that when someone trolls her, she slides into their DMs and sends them the number for the Samaritans. Stroke of genius if you ask me. Let's not dispel the notion that, however misguided, these cruel comments might be a cry for help from someone unable to correctly express their anger, sadness or fear. Because their trolling is rarely about you – it's about them, and what they feel they lack, or their own grief. They've probably been mean to ten other people that day. Hurt people tend to hurt people because they want to pass on the pain. Or maybe the person you are reminds them of the person they aren't. So, when dealing with trolls, that's what I find helpful to remember: it's not about me, it's about them.

## Remember real life

Given that social media is called social media, it's incredibly anti-social. I'm aware of so many young girls who are forward, charming, chatty and excited with me across social media, but then when we bump into each other at events, they are lacking the energy they possess online. There's a real divide between being active on social media and having an active social life and we cannot confuse the two. Try not to be so obsessed with your image on social media, or your relationships on social media, or your life on social media, that you forget to actually start living.

I'm guilty of this too. Some nights, I'll be out with friends, and I'm doing my third 'cheers!' Boomerang of the night, and my mates have a word, and say, 'Come on Vicky, put the phone down' – or I have to have a word with myself. There is nothing quite like being present with the people who mean the world to you, but it's easy to forget that in this new world we've created for ourselves. In this world, where if there isn't a photo for you to post on Instagram, you worry that other people – or even you – won't know it even happened, or how much fun you had, we've lost our sense of reality, of living in the moment, and what really matters. If it doesn't get a thousand likes, was it even worth it, we might foolishly ask ourselves. I think there's a fine line between using and abusing social media, and you must ask yourself if it's affecting your nights out, your holidays, your relationships and how present you are in all of those arenas. And if it is having a negative effect, admit you have an issue and take some time off.

My phone is my job, my life. I can easily convince myself I need it in my hands at all times, and that's part of my problem. My screen time is bloody terrifying! Be conscious of how much you're on it every day. Spend more time with people who make you forget to look at your phone. It's true you can tell who you're meant to spend your time with because you haven't checked your phone in an hour, and your sides hurt and your cheeks hurt from all the laughter. It's very easy in this day and age to think that if you're having a lot of fun everyone else needs to know about it, but what is actually important is that you're having such a good time that you forget to post about it. Once a year, I take a digital detox to get a bit of a reset. I only come off it for a few days, but taking a break helps my mental health.

Social media was invented to make us feel connected, but it's quickly become an addiction and a popularity contest. Be aware of how much time you're spending on social media and how it makes you feel and always, always remember that social media isn't necessarily real – it is a world filled with filters, good angles, editing apps, leased cars, designer clothes that people can't afford and the best bits of people's lives that they want you to see. The best of life exists beyond the things social media encourages us to crave. No one will remember how many Instagram followers you had or how sick your bikini pics were. They will remember you for the kindness you showed them and how you made them feel.

# The Secret To... a healthy relationship with social media

See perfectly curated, edited, filtered posts for what they are – and don't let envy or insecurity eat you up. When our brains get overloaded with other people's good news and perfect lives on these apps, our self-esteem can be damaged. Make a choice today to follow people who are honest, brave and empowering, who want to bring you up with them. Stop following people who make you feel envious, weak or unattractive. Seek out good news and good vibes only.

* Realise your power when you post. Appreciate that what you post can change someone's day – for better or worse. You can make your social media pages incredibly beautiful and positive, inspiring and affirmative. You can share your perceived flaws, which will help someone feel better about theirs. It takes real courage to share your vulnerabilities with the world, but it's only by speaking up that we can change negative dialogue around issues that harm us, and give others permission to do the same.

✳ Remember there is nothing wrong with taking a step back for a day, or taking a real break, for a week or a month – because your social media interaction should not define you. And remember, you can have millions of followers on social media, and still feel lonely. Nothing beats a board game night with your family, or a good gossip in person with your girls. Never get so caught up online that you forget to actually live.

✳ Four hours on Instagram today? I mean, I'm not judging you at all, mine is easily that every day. But think how else you could have utilised that time. You could have watched *The Kissing Booth One* and *The Kissing Booth Two* on Netflix, you could have made an amazing and super fancy dinner for your partner which gets you firmly out of the doghouse for all those sneaky Amazon Prime orders, you could have read half an awesome novel with a lush face mask on or cleaned your whole house and done the washing in that time. It's mind-blowing the number of hours of our day this tiny, insignificant little app consumes. If social media is your first choice to chill out that's absolutely fine, but be mindful of this: I read somewhere that most people post when they're happy and scroll mindlessly when they're sad – progressively making themselves feel sadder and more inadequate with every passing perfect image. I do this, we all do this – be sure that your social media usage hasn't become some sort of sadistic self-harm, and that when it does start to make you feel bad or inferior you get some space from it.

* Unless you must have your phone with you for a genuine reason, try leaving it behind or away from sight when you want/need to be engaged with those around you. Ban phones during meal times, read a magazine in the bath instead, switch it off in bed after a certain point, and leave it in the hotel room one day of your family holiday so you can fully escape. (NOTE TO SELF: Must try this one!!!)

* Remember – a cold, glaring phone screen cannot replace a warm hug, a shared giggle, a glass of wine with a friend, or eye-to-eye contact. Use social media to connect with friends and family, but don't let it replace them and your memory-making moments.

## PREPARE YOUR PURPOSE

Curate your feed so your social media activity doesn't mess with your positive and sassy energy. Write a list below of what you'd like your feed to look like and how you'd like the accounts you follow to make you feel. Do you want to feel inspired and motivated? Or maybe you just want something to make you laugh? Or holiday destination ideas? Research those voices and add them. Then make notes about what and who you don't want. If someone is constantly upsetting you, or stressing you out, or making you feel you're not good enough, don't be afraid to mute them, unfollow them or block them. Check your social media accounts and silence the voices who don't do the things on your first list.

What do you want your social media feed to look like?

_____

_____

_____

_____

What and who don't you want on your social
media feed?

_____

_____

_____

_____

Have I researched and followed the accounts that do
the things on my first list?                    ❏

Have I unfollowed, blocked or muted the accounts
that are the things on my second list?          ❏

# 8

# Smashing your career and looking to the future

*There is no limit on how much success there is to go round; we rise by lifting others — we sparkle infinitely more when we ask other women to join us in the sunshine.*

No one knows what the future holds, but we can take steps to get our hopes, dreams and goals moving in the direction we'd like. I have plenty. I wouldn't describe myself as a one-woman mogul, because that would make me sound like a self-absorbed dickhead, but I do have my fingers in a lot of pies, professionally speaking. Throughout my life, I've enjoyed watching and learning from remarkable women who have smashed their business goals, and built themselves strong networks of friends, family and colleagues — women who are happy to let other women shine and take their turn in the spotlight. Queens, basically. Queens who inspire and motivate me to build a better future.

When I was really young, I wanted to be like those

Disney princesses – which is one of the reasons I'm so happy that this new breed of princess is so strong and capable, and not just in desperate pursuit of a fella who couldn't recognise her once she took her makeup off and didn't have her fancy frock on (that's right, Prince Charming, I'm talking about you!). Moana, going out and doing it for herself. Anna in *Frozen*, powerful beyond measure and not after a bloke at all. Disney princesses were my first role models, then when I got a bit older, I wanted to be Victoria Beckham or Cheryl Cole, probably because of their infamous World Cup appearance back in 2006, when they completely stole the show with their super long extensions and incredibly skimpy shorts. I may have also been impressed by the fact that Victoria was married to David Beckham, but it wasn't just the fit husband that I aspired to have; they also had incredible careers. They were in girl bands, they were gorgeous, they sang cool songs in really cool outfits, and ran around shouting about girl power and being really sassy. What's not to love? After then of course, post-uni, came the Carrie Bradshaw phase.

Right now, who I look up to has changed again. I hugely admire my mam, who is a constant source of inspiration for me, and Michelle Obama because of how she stands up for herself and other people, boldly and bravely. It'll also come as no surprise to anyone who follows me on Instagram that I'm a bit of a royalist and I love the Queen. I feel like our Lizzie has given everything to our country over the years and, if *The Crown* is to be believed (and I do think some of it is), that hasn't always been easy. She is strong and resilient and has weathered many storms, and I truly believe she deserves our respect. I also love Kate Middleton – stylish, sweet, impossibly kind, and just seems like a really lovely woman as well as a good wife and mother. I've also been lucky enough when recording my podcast, The Secret To, to chat to some seriously incredible women, including Katherine Ryan and Giovanna Fletcher who inspire me huge amounts.

Now I'm going to say a controversial one and I know some of you reading this will cringe at my choice, but I don't think you can knock Kim Kardashian. Maybe an element of my admiration for her is because we both started in reality television, and that her start – like mine – was less than ideal. I'm referring, of course, to her sex tape – but let's forget that for a second and see her for what she really is: a self-made billionaire, a mother to four kids, one of the most easily recognisable women on the planet, who is running numerous businesses and also training to be a lawyer. I get very frustrated when people reduce her to one mistake she made – if, of course, the sex tape being released was a mistake and not a brilliant career move – fifteen years ago. It's the same kind of people who wish to reduce me to the mistakes I've made. I know I'm reaching here because Kim is obviously an internationally known billionaire and I'm obviously not, but I feel these people wish to reduce Kim and me because they're scared of a woman growing, evolving and achieving.

## Finding purpose, making progress

Whatever walk of life you're in, the path to success is never smooth. One of the best things I've learnt along the way is this: hitting rock bottom will teach you things that the mountaintops never will. I look back at times in my life when I was down on my luck, where I was struggling, when I'd made yet another huge mistake and things were beginning to look hopeless. And, actually, it was those moments that were the most pivotal in my life. They showed me what I was made of, allowed me to see who my real friends were, they taught me determination, strength and resilience. It's easy to be a nice person when you're on a high, but it's when you're on a low that life shows you and those around you who you really are, and what you're capable of. I don't regret the path my career has taken. If my career had been plain sailing, I'd have probably turned into a bit of an arsehole. I've met so many posh, rich people in my industry who grew up with everything, never having to struggle or think or worry, and they are, for the most part, incredibly entitled and deathly uninteresting. I'm pleased I've had the life I've had – filled with ups and downs and mistakes aplenty.

But there were definitely some pitfalls I wish I'd avoided. Finding the right people in my career to surround myself with has been a journey. The fame thing was brand new – no one in my family had done anything like this so they couldn't talk me through my choices, and I ended up kind of just bumbling my way through and learning by doing. I made a lot of bad decisions when I was younger for a number of reasons, but the biggest mistake was letting myself be influenced by the wrong kind of people. I put my trust in people that didn't have my best interests at heart, rather than in myself. I was incredibly naïve, and I didn't have a rulebook to follow. There were men who made me feel lesser to keep me weak and keep me subservient – to keep me down so they could stand taller, essentially. Another big mistake was misplaced loyalty. I know I stayed with some agents for longer than I should have. One of my first agents had me believe that there was nothing out there for me except *Geordie Shore* and if I left the show, I'd never be able to make anything of myself. I felt like they didn't care about me as a person, they just saw me as a cash cow, someone to gain or get something from. You've probably all had people like this in your life unfortunately, haven't you? People who you know aren't good influences, or are not invested in you for the right reasons, maybe people that you know are using or abusing you to get ahead.

Forgiveness has been a big thing for me. I can now forgive people *not* because I can see they're contrite or they've said sorry, or I know they've felt bad, or they're remorseful and have changed their behaviours, but for my own sake. To hold resentment in your heart, to feel hate and anger, to focus on the people who have done you wrong means you don't get to live a life of peace. And I deserve peace. And so do you. All of the bad boyfriends, the bad agents, the people who I worked with who tried to make me feel weak or take away my power, they don't get to own this next chapter, so I forgive them all. I can go forward with my head held high knowing all I did was love and trust – and put my faith in the wrong people. But they truly set out to diminish a woman's sparkle, and that is fucking sad. Please don't let anyone diminish your sparkle. In order to live the life you deserve you must have a light heart. A heart filled with hate and anger is heavy – so forgive and forget those who have hurt you and move forward with your life with hope and peace.

## Girl squad

When I left *Geordie Shore*, I took a big leap of faith. Everyone in my professional life was telling me I wouldn't amount to anything if I did, and making that decision meant there was no turning back with my agents. They chose to take on easy clients who were just happy to be on *Geordie Shore* – they were looking after the boys of the cast, and me – so me branching out would have made their lives a lot harder. Thankfully, at this point I met with the ladies who are still my agents today. Mokkingbird were these two incredibly strong young women starting up on their own, and that instantly got my attention. We've had our ups and downs, don't get me wrong, but I can't give them enough credit for taking a chance on me. One of their clients at the time didn't like that they were thinking of signing me and threatened, 'If you take her on, I'm leaving you,' and they told her straight that they saw huge potential in me, and they were going to bring me on board. She flounced off, and I'm now their longest standing client.

If you spoke to these agents now, they'd probably tell you our relationship is nigh on perfect. I have two women that look after me on a day-to-day basis, Gemma and Gem, and they are absolutely class. You know when I said in the friendship chapter that you are who you spend your time with? Well – even though they are technically my colleagues, we've definitely become close and have that bond. Gemma is a mum and a wife, and is totally smashing her career. If I'm half as happy as her in a few years' time I'll be pleased as punch. And

Gem is a total ray of sunshine; nothing fazes her. You can tell her you're lost when you're due on live television in fifteen minutes and she'll just calmly say 'Leave it with me' and sort everything out with no drama. The pair of them have really impressed on me the values we need to hold onto, which is hard in this business: hard work, punctuality, politeness and conscientiousness.

They've really helped me get my head around how things are done in showbusiness, despite the weird dynamic between an agent and a client. I know the relationship between a lot of agents and clients is more business-orientated and straightforward – you are a commodity, after all, and you're how they make money – but through mutual honesty, openness and respect, we've evolved that dynamic and we now have so much more than that. I can't say this enough to you: treat people how you want to be treated, personally and professionally. Again, remember – you match energies. If you are optimistic, kind and respectful, even if the person opposite you is having the worst day, they'll smile back. It takes a really special kind of dickhead not to smile back. I'm so grateful for how they've grafted, hustled and protected me over the years. I know I am one very lucky little bug.

It's like any relationship you have with a colleague or a boss or someone in your team – you have to work at it, it has to be nurtured. I truly believed when I was younger that part of my 'brand' was telling it like it is, which was very childish. Honesty is great, but when it's served without a side of tact, it's just rudeness. I used to be the bullish and headstrong person with zero tact, which made for really awkward working environments, so I've definitely upped my diplomacy skills. Everybody is doing a job and bringing something to the table, and nobody is more important than anybody else. It doesn't matter if you're the talent, or the boss, or the one who makes the tea – it takes a village to make something wonderful happen, and no one cog is needed in a wheel more than any other. I've learnt to be gracious, respectful and hardworking – three traits everyone should take into their place of work.

## Learn to listen

Being aware of other people's thoughts and feelings is crucial, too. Being a good listener is key in the workplace. Someone told me a while ago that too many people listen to reply, not listen to understand, and once I heard that, it became almost impossible for me to talk to someone without trying to work out which they were. It's a fun little game to have with people. Some people just listen because they're waiting for you to stop so they can start talking about themselves. I totally appreciate that some people just don't have those social skills, but there are people who should know better. I don't like to use the word hate, but I hate them! I just think, *why are you here? This isn't a conversation; you could be talking to a potted plant and it's pointless.* A conversation is someone sharing stories, sharing secrets, solving problems and bonding. If you're only interested in your own voice and opinions, and you're not listening to understand, you could be talking to a chicken Kiev. If you just want to screech at something, don't do it at me. And don't let people do it to you, either. Yes, often it's arrogant people, or people who consider their opinion more important than anyone else's, and sometimes it's insecure people, who are nervously trying to impress you. It's up to you how you want to deal with these types of listeners. I've given them a lot of grace over the years, shown a lot of patience, and I still have a few of them in my life. I give them far too much leeway and can tell they're not all interested in what I'm saying and are just waiting impatiently for their turn to take over. I am working on being more assertive and ridding my life of these people, but it takes time. And ultimately, I'm such a soft touch.

I don't think there's any place for egos in any walk of life. I believe self-confidence and a belief in who you are is important and strong, but ego is weak. I don't mean to make a sweeping generalisation, *buuuut* ... the biggest egos I've encountered all belong to men. Now being thirty-three, very long in the tooth, and knowing what I want, I try to avoid those people, and if I ever find myself in a professional situation with an egomaniac, I don't stay for long. Being arrogant doesn't automatically make them a bad person. As I said, they could be insecure, they could be intimidated by you – and if you wanted to psychoanalyse it you could almost take their chatting away about their achievements, cars and homes, etc. as a compliment because they're trying to impress you. But what it all boils down to is this: we all have a very limited amount of time here. Do you want to spend your coveted free time laughing and sharing with people you love and respect, or do you want to spend your life with some dickhead banging on about his achievements? Completely not! Now, whether it's work-based or personal, I keep my interactions with these people to a bare minimum.

## The in crowd

Over time, whatever career you're in, you realise whose opinion of you is important, and whose is not. When I was younger, I didn't think I could learn anything from anyone, which I know is just a characteristic of being young. As I got older, I've realised every day is a school day, and I can learn something from absolutely everybody. That's where I'm at now, which is so moved on from where I used to be, super defensive and unable to take criticism from anyone else. I remember when older people used to try and offer advice I used to think, *what the fuck can they teach me, they're not living my life?*, and dismiss what they were saying and their good intentions immediately. But actually, lots of people are facing different things and learning lessons every single day. It doesn't matter if their situation isn't exactly the same as yours, there could be ideas and themes and solutions that might resonate with you. You just become so much more open to learning, improving and being better. I used to think I had it all figured out, and now I realise none of us have. None of us! And that's half the fun and the beauty of life.

My god, do I want to be Holly Willoughby in ten years' time? Yes please! Do I want to do all the amazing things Davina McCall is doing? Yes! Do I want to be Tess Daly? Wey Aye! But I have to understand that in order to get there, I have to get better. And in order to get better – in order for any one of us to get better in our chosen field – we have to practise, we have to learn, we have to show up on time ready to work hard, and we have to be willing to take advice from others who have been there, done it and got the T-shirt.

## Bold and brave

I know I have to be unafraid to take risks in my career, but it's still super daunting. There is still so much I do every day that scares me. Sometimes I take on the challenge and smash it and I have a great time and I feel like I've acquired a new talent, and sometimes I'm crap at it and I've just got to live with that. I have those moments when I've tried something brave and new and I hate it, and decide I don't want to do it anymore, and that's fine, because I gave it a go. No regrets. I really believe living with that feeling that you should have given something a go but didn't – that regret – is far worse than just trying and being a bit rubbish. At least you gave it a shot, and you know if it's good or bad. Awareness is power. Especially self-awareness.

For example, when I did *Celebrity MasterChef*, everyone thought I'd be kicked out the first week – even my agents did. No one believed I could cook, not even me, because I lived off takeaways. Well, I was fresh off a break-up as well, so I was devoid of confidence and feeling vulnerable. So I completely agreed with everything everyone was saying, that I'd be crap, I'd be toast very fast – no pun intended. But something miraculous happened – I thrived. There was something so soothing and lovely about the methodical rhythm of following a recipe, and even though I was a headless chicken running around the kitchen, inside I was serene and becoming better at something new. It restored my faith in myself and my abilities and I realised I wasn't useless or worthless, like being cheated on had made me feel. And under this new blossoming confidence I began to flourish as a strong, confident woman.

Now, conversely, in 2020 I did *SAS: Who Dares Wins* and it was the worst mistake of my life. Everyone warned me not to do it. And I ignored them. I have always been relatively physically fit, but coming straight off the back of two national lockdowns and sitting on my arse for the best part of a year was not the best preparation for what is widely acknowledged to be the toughest show on television. I wanted to be pushed out of my comfort zone, and I wanted a challenge. And that was exactly what I got. There was not one moment of recording that show when I thought, *I'm smashing this.* Not one moment where I thought, *this is going to change me for the better!* We were up the top of Scotland, on the Isle of Skye, and the terrain was awful. I sprained my ankle on the first day and had to keep going. No one gives anyone any sympathy – it's absolutely savage. Even the fella who strapped it up for me just said, 'Yeah, that's a bad sprain that, but you'll live.' Of course, these guys have been through so much worse, so they don't have sympathy for anyone – especially not some entitled celeb who's hurt her little foot on the first day. The entire time I was recording I just thought *I'm cold, I'm wet, and if that man shouts at me again I'm going to tear him a new one!* I hated it. Looking back, a year later, I can tell myself I was brave. And one moment of insane bravery can change your life. Even if you don't end up getting enrolled in the SAS, I learnt something: that I never wanted to do it again. Oh, and one other lesson it taught me: I've spent ten years working out what makes me happy, what I need and what I don't, and after spending four days up there with those fellas in Scotland, being shouted and screamed at, I knew I hadn't worked this hard for so long to be made to feel that miserable. I learnt that I'm now in such a strong place of happiness and confidence, that I will not let anyone drag me back.

## Swimming with sharks

I am, at the moment, struggling with my identity. I know I probably look like I've got it all figured out, but for years I've been Vicky from reality TV – whether it was *Ex on the Beach* or *Celebrity Coach Trip*, everyone knows me from that realm. But what I want to be is Vicky the Television Presenter. Vicky the Respected Author. Vicky the Valued Broadcaster. Eventually, I want people to be more interested in the quality of my work than the details of my life. It's a difficult jump to make because there is a huge stigma around people who come from reality television, basically that we're talentless and have nothing to offer. We're superficial, vapid, unintelligent, and all we're good for is flogging outfits or whitening products. I resent those implications. I don't agree with those statements, but they've followed me my whole life. I've played with the idea of being better, and every so often I will try something that takes me to that next level, but then I get scared. And I run back.

My life coach gave me this analogy about being brave enough to form the identity you want, really reaching for your dreams instead of just talking about them. Here's the analogy: at the moment, you're on a desert island. It's a little island but it's comfortable and you know every inch of it. You know which parts to avoid because there's quicksand, and you know where the good coconuts grow. It's your island. You are queen of that island. Why would you want to leave it? Well, because in the distance you can see another island. And it looks bigger. You don't know anything about it, but you just feel like it could be better – there could be less quicksand, bigger coconuts. There could be hot fellas that look like the Rock's character Maui from *Moana*, and there could be more fish! So you start swimming, full of hope and promise, because you're feeling stagnant on your island and you're motivated by the thought of something better in the distance. But the minute the sea gets choppy, the minute the sky gets dark, you start to panic and turn back to what you know, the same quicksand and the same coconuts. Because back there, where you came from, you know what to expect, which makes you feel comfortable and safe. And being safe and comfortable is nice ...

But you don't grow in safe and comfortable. You

don't make your dreams come true in safe and comfortable. Now, I'm halfway between reality television Vicky and the Vicky who hasn't quite got a face yet. The Vicky who hasn't quite taken form. I know she's out there and she can do it, and I know it's going to be better for me, but I also know the water is dark and choppy, and there might be sharks. I'm nervous, and fearful, but I'm not going to stop, and if you have big dreams for a different, better, bolder life, you shouldn't stop trying to reach them either. I don't want to live the rest of my life on this island, the island that is safe and comfortable, and I don't want any of you to feel like you haven't swum after your dreams and ambitions in pursuit of happiness either.

Yes, I love getting out of my comfort zone, but I am scared about this next chapter, just like all of you who are contemplating your next step or making changes in your life right now. Have faith. Be brave. I would say to anyone who has goals, and is struggling to proactively get what they want, or even work out what it is they want, do a vision board. I swear by them. I have two in my office, two huge ones, one for my professional life and one for my personal life. I'm not scared to tell you what's on them. My professional one is filled with images of me on *Strictly Come Dancing*, and the BBC logo, and it's got a picture of Stacey Dooley, because I want to film hard-hitting documentaries and talk about issues that I'm passionate about, like women's reproductive health, women's safety and so many other issues that affect us. I want to lift the lid on serious things. It's got a picture of Heart radio studios, because I really want to be a radio presenter. And it has photos of clothing ranges, magazine covers, books and everything that I could possibly think of that I want to tick off my bucket list. When I see it every day, it reminds me why I'm working so hard. It's easier to make small steps to your bigger goals when you're constantly reminded what those bigger goals are. Now, if I'm about to post something on Instagram, I think, *is this going to serve me in the long run? Is it showing me being honest and real, passionate and positive?* All the things I want to be known for. I look at it and think, *are other women going to gain something from it, or will other decision makers look at it and think I'd be a great ambassador for their brand or a great face for their television or radio show?*

My personal mood board is a lot more difficult for me. I feel like I've made great strides in my career over the years, but I don't feel like I've really moved on personally. I always found my lack of personal success a great source of shame and embarrassment. I felt embarrassed that I couldn't make a man love me, make a man treat me right or make a relationship work. Obviously, I know now I couldn't 'make' someone love me, and even if I could I wouldn't want that – I want someone to want to love me, be excited to be with me and be as invested in our relationship as I am. This thought process tortured me for a really long time until very recently, when I've begun to realise there is no real timeline that we have to follow. There is no personal checklist with a bunch of boxes that all have to be ticked off by a certain age. Women are especially guilty of putting this unnecessary pressure on ourselves, and it only leads to stress and heartache. I can't tell you how many times I've felt like I was drowning in disappointment and despair and feelings that I just don't quite measure up because I'm not married and don't have kids. For years, I've been ashamed of my personal achievements. For years, people have said what's been the happiest moment of your life, and I'd have to say winning the jungle. And I felt so sad that I couldn't say that I was getting married, or having a baby. Finally, now I hope I am taking great big strides in terms of my personal life. I've stopped settling for just any form of affection, I've stopped trying to fix people, I've stopped trying to heal people. I understand that I am not a rehabilitation centre for broken men. I've searched for someone who improves me, and who loves me not in spite of all of my flaws, but because of them.

I'm heading in the right direction with my love life finally. I'm being kinder to myself and accepting that if marriage is on the cards for me, that's amazing. And if kids are on the cards, brilliant. But if those two things aren't, I'll survive – there's lots of other ways to have a happy and full life. We need to normalise accepting different types of end games for women. If you want to be married by twenty-five and have ten kids and be a stay-at-home mam, that is amazing and so beautiful. If you want to dominate the boardroom, smash your professional life and live with your partner with no other commitment, that is a boss bitch move and super empowering. If you want to travel the world with your best friends, feeling sand between your toes, kissing new boys in new countries every month, staying single and fabulous, that is progressive and special and you are amazing. All of these scenarios are perfectly wonderful ways to live your life to the fullest. We need to stop assuming that the only way a woman could possibly be happy is if she has a husband by the time she's thirty and a tribe of tiny love terrorists hanging from her tits. Okay?

I am one of those girls who wants to be married, wants a big wedding, wants to be loved. And I suppose that's why my personal mood board has been such a difficult one for me, because it's never changed. Whereas my professional one has evolved, and I've added pictures as my confidence has grown and who I am as a person has evolved, or I have taken off pictures of things that I've achieved, I felt my personal board had stalled. When you're still staring at the same picture of a wedding dress, you can feel a little bit demoralised. And I think that is natural. I think

I've stopped beating myself up over not being married or having kids, because if I'd have married or had kids with any of those men I'd previously been going out with, been engaged to, or thought I'd end up with, I'd be divorced by now. None of us were right for each other. I think finally now I'm able to look at my personal mood board and not feel like a disappointment to myself and everyone else around me. For years the top things on there were to get a puppy and buy a new house, which I had to move hell and high water to make happen, but it finally happened. I still want the same things I always did. I do really want to be married, but not just to anybody, which I kind of did before. I want to be married to Ercan.

## Future mama?

That girl on *Loose Women* seven years ago, who felt woefully unprepared to be pontificating about childbirth and motherhood, marriage, divorce and everything in between, that girl who was just figuring herself out, was brave to admit she didn't yet know if she wanted to be a parent. As women, we're still made to feel there's something wrong with us if we don't yearn to be a mother. And for the longest part of my life, I didn't want kids; they really weren't on my radar. It's only now that I'm thirty-three and in a loving relationship that something has clicked. I think it clicks for lots of us when we get older, doesn't it?

Motherhood doesn't have to be the end goal for every woman, but it is for lots of my friends. They all have this burning desire to be a mama. I'm still figuring that part of my life out, I think. Some days I really want children and I can't imagine what my life would be without a busy, noisy house filled with children's laughter, but other days I love my life, I love my job and can't imagine slowing down for even a second; I love our freedom and I do sometimes think maybe I'm just meant to be a dog mama to Milo. A while ago I got pretty obsessed with the idea of being a mother, and part of me thinks I was obsessed with the idea of children because I didn't think it would be possible when I split up with my last boyfriend. There I was starting again from scratch at thirty-one, and I knew it would take a year to find someone, a year getting to know them, then two years having fun getting engaged and married – and that's if it all works out – and I'd be thirty-five before I started trying to have a baby. I worried it would be too late, but of course it doesn't have to be. That was just the irrational fear of a woman who's been conditioned to think she needs to have her life all neatly wrapped up in a bow and sorted by the time she's thirty.

I want women to talk about the pressure we feel to be mothers, and the timeline other people hold us to, how we're often conditioned to think getting married and becoming a mother should all happen before you turn thirty. I remember a girl in my industry being asked about my success. The interviewer said something like, 'Aren't you proud of her?' and she replied, 'Well, yes, but when I'm Vicky's age I hope I'm focusing on having a husband and kids!' And if that's her opinion, that's fine, but I felt like I was getting career-shamed, and it was sexist. It's so archaic, this idea that we can only be happy or successful if we're hitched to someone and popping out babies.

But I let it get into my head, and I let these opinions convince me that I wasn't *really* successful because I was missing the crucial parts that other women and society told me I needed to feel whole. And some women aren't made to be mothers. Some women are made to be badass CEOs who break balls and manage a staff of 300; some women are meant to be professional sportswomen and have loads of different partners. We can do whatever we want – it's your beautiful, unique path, so choose the one you want, don't get bogged down with everyone else's idea of what is right. You don't need to impress these women. Take the path you want, be you, but please don't, whatever you do, shame any other woman for taking a different path to you, or having a different dream to you. Some women don't want children, some women can't have children. This doesn't make them any less of a woman.

It's about time we got over the idea that to be content as women we have to have kids. Kids are on my personal vision board, but there's still a question mark above them. Don't get me wrong, the idea of tiny Ercans makes my ovaries scream, because he's so fricking cute. And I think if I had a little boy like him, he'd be so kind and lovely I'd just want to squish him constantly. But then I consider the possibility of a little me, and I am terrified to the depths of my very soul. Loud, impossibly inquisitive, full of energy, refusing to sleep ... if you think these qualities were something I developed over time you'd be painfully wrong. I've been this way since I was a child, and according to my poor mother it was incredibly exhausting. Some days I wake up and think, *yes please, kids, I'd be a good mam*, and sometimes I wake up and acknowledge there is so much more that I still need to do for myself first.

I've given up making myself feel bad because I don't have it all figured out – and you need to be done with that too. It's the twenty-first century. We're allowed to want different things. We're allowed to give people grace when they make different decisions to you. I think we need to understand that everyone is different. What works for them might not work for you. Variety makes life more interesting. If everyone wanted to be a Type A high performer, it wouldn't work. It takes everyone to make the world go round – it takes home-makers, bad bitch bosses, nurses, teachers, it takes us all. Once you stop comparing yourself to others, or trying to make everyone see everything your way, you'll be happier. Embrace your own journey, and encourage others to embrace theirs.

Because my professional life is so intrinsically linked to my personal life I really struggle with balance, and for years I've made public knowledge so much of my life that probably should have been kept more personal and private. Finding fame through reality television made me struggle to draw the line. Balance is still a double-edged sword. Because I'm open and honest, and so much of my personal life makes its way onto social media, is the reason so many people seem to really like me. I don't want to stop it, but I do have to get better at keeping something for myself. For many years, I truly believed the reason I'd stayed where I was for so long was because people liked me, and it is! I'm not talented. I can't kick a football, sing a song or do a great dance. I'm rubbish at all that. My income is based on my likeability. So I feel so grateful for people voting for me in the jungle, buying things I promote, and following me on Instagram. I feel beholden to them. It is a pressure.

I think when I was struggling to be someone I wasn't – glamorous, bright-eyed, bushy-tailed and perfectly coiffed every day – it put me under an extreme amount of pressure. Now I'm warts-and-all Vicky, there's less pressure, and I do love the approach I've taken to my image and social media. I haven't got it all figured out; who among us has? There's so many days when I overshare, and I get a phone call from my agents telling me off. 'Courtney Cox follows you now on social media, Vicky, we've all had a chat in the office and decided that it's about time you stopped posting pictures of your toenail falling off,' was how one recent conversation went. Loose lips sink ships, and I'm totally capable of that every so often.

## Act on your ambition

There is a myth that as you get older that you're supposed to want less and become complacent, but I truly disagree with that. The older I get, and the more secure I become, the more I realise what I want and how far I'm willing to go to get those things. When you're younger, you're scared of trying new things because you think everyone is watching you and expecting you to fail, but as you get older your self-awareness and self-acceptance grows, and although you know you won't be great at everything all the time, you know you owe it to yourself to give it a shot. You learn that everyone might not like you, and that's okay. That's true confidence. I'd love to debunk the myth that you have to do less as you age; there is no age limit on ambition. I remember reading that Alan

Rickman didn't get his first role in a film until he was forty-one. There are so many people out there thinking, *I'd love to be a travel agent but I'm scared to retrain*, or *I'd love to go back to college now my kids are a bit older but I probably wouldn't get a place*, or thinking – knowing – they are in the wrong job but deciding, *I'm here now, I better not rock the boat*. Bollocks! It's never too late to change your career, go back to school, kick up your heels and decide you want to move to another country and marry a matador.

You're allowed to do whatever you want, and this idea you just have to stop at a certain age and settle for what you've got in life, it was probably designed by a man to keep you small. Don't ever be afraid to chase the dreams and the things you want, because life only stops being exciting when you stop trying. Your dreams have no expiry date. Push your boundaries, get out of your comfort zone, do something scary, be brave – because a split second of courage has the power to change your whole life. No regrets, remember.

Yes, I've got a basket full of mistakes, grazed knees and toppled-over hurdles behind me, but it's all led me to be who I am right here, right now. If I hadn't made mistakes on *Geordie Shore*, I wouldn't have the career I have. If I didn't get sacked from some shows, the doors wouldn't have opened on others. Your mistakes are part of your story – they probably make up some of the more interesting chapters, with the more interesting characters. Never forget that.

## You are allowed to be loud

Don't be ashamed to have a purpose, and go for it. Aim for your ambitions, desires and dreams – men aren't afraid to have them, neither should we girls. This isn't 1950. You don't have to stop at making a home and having a baby. If you want to, good. But if you don't, that's okay too. You are allowed to be loud, you are allowed to be demanding, you are allowed to be strong, you are allowed to be whatever the fuck you want to be. And that's what's so beautiful about being a woman today. We're fed up with being told what we want, and now we're going for it all. Who's with me?

# The Secret To... being the master of your own destiny

* Remember you are the master of your own destiny. This is your life, and we only get one shot at it, so try and care less what other people think and do things YOUR way.

* Do things every day that keep you on the right track, a track that you control at your own pace. You're not in a race, and you don't need to worry about who is ahead and who is behind. What are you doing for you? Keep a note of simple, small things that make each day better: are you getting enough water, moving your body, communicating with people who make you feel strong?

* And just in case no one has told you this in the last twenty-four hours, remember: you're doing great – life isn't always easy or fun, but you're making the most of what you have right now to build a better future.

* You look amazing – don't pick yourself apart, bring yourself up. Remember the positive

self-talk task in Chapter 2 – make sure you're still doing it. Talking to yourself how you'd talk to a friend – with kindness, positivity and empathy.

* You are powerful beyond measure, remember. You can do more than you even know you are capable of. You just need to believe in yourself – and put in some hard work.

* You are the boss of your own body. You can say no, say yes, and love and value it without permission from a partner. You are also the boss of your own mind, your own goals, your own dreams – and your own timeline. You have the power.

* Today can be whatever you make it. Shine bright and encourage everyone you meet to be the shiniest, best version of themselves, too. Queen behaviour right there!

## PREPARE YOUR PURPOSE

Sometimes it's really hard to focus on what you want, and to keep a tight grip on what your goals are, but when you have them there in front of you, visually, you can't lose sight of who you want to be and where you want to end up. The images are there and so are your dreams, right in front of your face. Crafting yourself a board full of empowering photos and words and placing it somewhere you'll see it every day is proven to help motivation levels. Make a start in the space below, and jot down some of the stuff you want it to include. You could try making lists under different sections, e.g. for me, for my home, career, adventures. I once read somewhere that you are 80 per cent more likely to achieve your goals if you write them down. I have absolutely no idea if it's true or not, but I can only assume that if you add pictures to that you whack on another 10 per cent. Seems logical, right? Regardless of the probably incorrect statistics I am feeding you here, one thing is for certain: visual reminders of your purpose will help you stay on track.

My mood

board

# Epilogue

*Don't spend so long counting other people's sprinkles*
*that you let your ice cream melt.*

I've gone through a huge amount of growth over the last decade. There've been some incredibly upsetting and difficult lows, like losing my best friend, losing my grandma and getting my heart broken, and there've been some truly wonderful highs, like leaving *Geordie Shore* and winning the jungle. I can look back on these things now that enough time has elapsed, and appreciate how beautiful some of those moments were, and acknowledge that others are still really painful to remember. But life is about the ebbs and flows, the ups and downs, the joy and the agony. In order to learn, grow and become a better version of yourself you *have* to make mistakes. Making mistakes is part of the process of growing as a human being. We need to acknowledge this, accept it and normalise it.

This is what I really need you to get into your

head – and heart – as you finish reading this book: without the dark, you won't appreciate the light. In order to be a well-rounded, interesting, courageous person you have to have known hardships, to have walked through life at its rock bottom, learning difficult lessons, knowing that one day you'll be back up on the mountaintops. You know, each time I messed up, made a mistake or was feeling lost and low, people used to say to me, 'You'll look back on this one day, and think *I'm so glad he cheated on me* or *I'm so glad I didn't get that job*,' and I remember thinking at the time, *what do they know? Who were they to tell me how I would feel?* Now I know my reaction was because I was angry, and part of me, each time I was in the deep, dark valley, thought I would never breathe fresh air and feel the sun on my face again. I believed I'd never stop hurting, never stop reeling from the pain.

Well, here I am three years down the line from my broken heart and my cancelled wedding, having to move into my thirties and start all over again. And you know what? I am so glad my ex-fiancé fucked up. I look at who I am now, and I know I'm stronger. I also know if things don't work out in my love life, I'll be fine on my own. Yes, it was a painful way to learn that, but over the last ten years, I've crammed a lot of living in, and I'm ready to face anything life throws at me, whether it be setbacks and failures or triumphs and achievements. I am ready to nurture my personal life a bit more; I want to give as much time to my relationships and happiness as I have my professional life. I'm ready for a slightly slower pace of life. I don't know what's around the corner, but I know I live every day in a way that will allow me to deal with what comes up. I surround myself with good people and treat them how I would like to be treated. I work hard, I look after my mind and my body, and I know that if something painful does come up – if I don't get the job I desperately wanted, or if everything goes away tomorrow and I lose my fancy house, or I can't have kids – I know that I will be okay, regardless. Because that's what happens when you walk through fire and come out the other side stronger. You realise you are made of steel and nothing will break you.

## A different decade

Turning thirty was a momentous milestone for me. Loads of people tell you it's hard, getting older. That after you've turned thirty having a hangover will be as hard to recover from as minor surgery; that wrinkles will start filling your face while your natural collagen deserts you; that your biological clock will start ticking at an alarming rate. People who have already turned thirty can't wait to fill your head with all this negative, dreary bullshit. But what they miss out is the incredibly liberating feeling you get when you finally hit thirty and stop doubting yourself so much. Once my life settled, I felt more relaxed, more accepting. More comfortable in my own skin, I believed I was truly capable of anything. Every time I put on a swimsuit in my twenties, I used to worry about what everyone would think of me and panic that I didn't have the perfect body. Now I put on a swimsuit and I don't care what anyone else sees. I see a body that has got me through thirty-odd years of life pretty well, that has seen me climb mountains, conquer jungles and get me through a global pandemic. I am the shape I am, and I have boobs and a bum, and squishy bits too, and I'm done fighting my body, I'm done apologising for it. Now I just accept who I am. Dare I say I love who I am? I'm done fighting my metabolism. I'm done fighting my personality too. I'm done trying to hide the fact that I'm a woman with ambition and drive. I'm done trying to make myself want to be a mother when the time isn't right. I'm accepting of who I am and it's the most liberating feeling ever. And here's the great secret: once you accept yourself, you can start to love yourself. I know I am brash, opinionated and desperate to be liked all the time – that's just me. Confidence is not thinking everyone is going to like you, it's knowing you will be okay if they don't. Liberate yourself from the opinions of others and watch the magic of your life unfold.

Transparency and authenticity are two key things

we should all try to build into our day-to-day lives. We need to realise that showing our scars is a good thing to do. We're all so desperate to not be seen as vulnerable, emotional and weak – three insults that have been traditionally used to keep women down. Actually, sharing those things makes you brave, strong and real. Since going through those tough life events that robbed me of the energy to be a fake, impossibly strong and permanently together woman, I've found a real sense of pride in myself. I'm a survivor, and I'm a supporter of other women. Those are two things that make me powerful beyond my wildest imagination.

## Rebel love

Self-love is the biggest act of anarchy you can do; to get into the mindset where you don't care if you don't fit into anyone else's box, and you don't care if you don't look the way other people want you to look or do things when they tell you it's time to do them. It's all about you and giving yourself time and respect. Learning to love yourself isn't easy, in fact I'd go as far as to say that the journey to self-love and self-acceptance is one of the hardest and longest out there and none of us have everything all figured out. But I know this much – learning to love yourself doesn't come from losing loads of weight or finding a fella. It comes from surviving the low points in your life. It comes from accepting your mistakes and learning from them. And then one day, you just wake up and you realise that you are fierce and strong and full of fire, and that not even you can hold yourself back because your passion burns brighter than your fears. (I unfortunately can't take credit for that one; I believe it's Mark Antony, but whoever said it, they are bang on.)

Do you want to be sixty or eighty years old and realise you've wasted the vast majority of your life not liking yourself? Imagine the things you could achieve if every morning, when you looked in the mirror, you said or thought something nice about yourself instead of pulling yourself down for not being perfect? Tell yourself you've got great eyes, or good skin, or that the body you're pulling apart gave you children or got you through a global pandemic. Tell yourself anything, just make sure it's nice. Because we're all perfectly imperfect and fabulously flawed, and that's what makes each of us special. You can achieve incredible things – once you stop convincing yourself you can't or you don't deserve them. We must stop shrinking to make other people feel better about themselves. Instead of shrinking, shine ... shine so bright that in turn other people feel encouraged to shine too.

Would you like to know what makes me hopeful for the future? I was miserable ten years ago. I didn't like the way I looked, I didn't like many of the people in my life, I didn't like the place I was in mentally or physically, I didn't like my job. And I look at everything I've done since that point of misery, and especially since I turned thirty, and I feel immense pride. I'm happy now, and I made it happen. You can say I'm lucky, and that I was just in the right place at the right time. People can say whatever they want to me to try to diminish my achievements, and believe me they have tried, but it was me who made sure I was happy. And if I'm this happy at thirty-three, can you imagine how happy I am going to be at forty-three? The possibilities are bloody endless. I decided to change my narrative and you can change yours too. If you don't like where you're at, who you're becoming or where you're headed, *you* have the power to change it. Never forget that you are the master of your own destiny and *you* get to decide who you become. That fills me with hope, and I hope it gives you hope too. Because if I can do it, anyone can.

Remember, happiness isn't a permanent state. Happiness is not an end destination. Happiness isn't constant.

Life cannot be rainbows, kittens and candy floss every day, because if it was you wouldn't appreciate it. You can be happy despite regrets, shadows and skeletons. The people who own their regrets, shadows and skeletons are the best kind of people, if you ask me. They're the ones you want to sit next to at a dinner party – the one with histories and back stories, struggles and strife, grazed knees and endless anecdotes. There *are* going to be chapters of your book that you don't really want to read out loud, and that's okay, but don't be ashamed of them, because they made you who you are and they do not have to define you. And maybe one day, you'll write them all down and pop them in a book like me, and some woman will read them and take solace in knowing that she wasn't alone in her mistake or moment of weakness. And wouldn't that be nice?

Everyone's version of happiness looks different, and that's okay. It's drilled into us as women that we can only be happy if we have a husband and children but, as I've said many times in this book, that is not everyone's idea of happiness. Whether you want to travel the world with your girlfriend, settle down in your hometown with your first love, excel in your professional life and have a shit load of cats, or if you want to have it all – the job, the house, the husband, the cats and the kids – go for it and own it. Take no notice of what other people are doing. Comparison truly is the thief of joy. Instead, focus on you and your happiness and the rest will flow.

Happiness is subjective, so never be afraid to

embrace your unique take on it, I urge you. You are not doing anything wrong. Everyone is different. Stop looking around you at what other people are doing, appreciate what you have and embrace the incredibly special journey you're on, because I really don't want your ice cream to melt while you're busy counting other people's sprinkles.

# Acknowledgements

I don't even know where to start with these acknowledgments. There are so many people I want to thank for making this book possible and I'm really scared I leave someone out!

First and foremost, I have to thank my lovely editor Nicky Crane – who believed in this book so much and fought to make it a reality. I'm really grateful to you, Nick! And everyone at Little, Brown for supporting my literary endeavours: Thalia Proctor in editorial, Millie Seaward for all her work on publicity, Brionee Fenlon for marketing, Marie Hrynczak in production, and everyone in sales that helped to get this book out there. Thanks also to Rhys Timson, Louise Harvey and Josephine Cox for making the audiobook happen.

Next, I have to thank my talented and incredibly patient ghostwriter Sarah Ivens – without whom, this book would be very different. Thank you, Sarah, for allowing me to be so honest and open with you – we knew you were the woman for the job from that very first Zoom call.

Next up I have to thank my long-suffering agents at Mokkingbird! Gemma Wheatley and Gem-Joy Allan: you guys are the best and have stood by me through thick and thin and without your belief that I had something worth saying, I don't think I would have believed it myself. Thank you for never giving up on me. Thank you also to my literary agent, Lauren Gardner, to James Delamare at Dundas Communications for helping with PR, and to the podcast team at Spirit Studios for supporting the book.

Next I'd like to acknowledge my beautiful friends, family and partner – without your love guidance and downright gorgeousness I wouldn't be the person I am today; who knows if I'd even be here. I love you and will never be able to thank you enough.

And finally, I'd like to say a big, big thank you to anyone who has supported me throughout my career: voted for me when I was in the jungle, wrote something kind about me on Instagram, listened to my podcast or bought this book. You guys are the best and I'll be eternally grateful to you all forever.